EX
PAN
SIONS

T0352126

Edited by
Hashim Sarkis and
Ala Tannir

La Biennale di Venezia

PRESIDENT
Roberto Cicutto

BOARD
Luigi Brugnaro
Vice President

Claudia Ferrazzi
Luca Zaia

AUDITORS' COMMITTEE
Jair Lorenco
President

Stefania Bortoletti
Anna Maria Como

DIRECTOR GENERAL
Andrea Del Mercato

**ARTISTIC DIRECTOR
OF THE
ARCHITECTURE DEPARTMENT**
Hashim Sarkis

CONTENTS

Expansions

Architecture is the furniture of time, William Faulkner once observed. His metaphor delved into the anachronistic nature of architecture as it relates to the present, and its role in arranging and anticipating the possibilities of the future while registering, like furniture, the passage of time. That such an observation comes from a novelist rather than an architect does not make it any less relevant. It is deeply architectural. It expands the typological understanding of architecture, as form that outlives the conditions that brought it into being. It also grows the repertoire of architectural imagery: if architects are the upholsterers of time, those who arrange and rearrange in anticipation of different possibilities of inhabitation, then what about the architectural equivalent of the groove left in the rug by the leg of the couch, long after the couch has been moved?

The collection of texts in this book broadens the architectural imaginary by expanding the medium of La Biennale di Venezia's 17th International Architecture Exhibition from the drawing and model to the essay. It also expands the range of viewpoints from those of the architect to those looking at architecture as a means to inspire the pursuit of imagining how we can live together, both within the field and outside of it. Along the way, the book elaborates on the agency of architecture.

The essays embrace the theme of the exhibition and the invitation to include other voices in thinking the question of living together, and their authors articulate their responses through architecture, even though not (always) as architects.

The architectural project is the primary mode of participation in the Biennale. Whether presented in the form of drawings, models, or installations, these projects invariably emphasize the material and visual forms of architectural representation and the projected nature of architecture—that it projects possibilities for what could be. As radical as they may be in imagining new possibilities, the projects in the exhibition maintain a well-accepted allographic relationship between forms of architectural representation and architectural form itself.

Guided and convened by the open question, *How Will We Live Together?*, around which this entire undertaking—in the galleries, on paper, and beyond—revolves, the responses in this book are naturally personal to their authors. Each of them reveals a different understanding of architecture and a different perception of its stakes. Yet, unsurprisingly, overlapping thoughts and subjects emerge, as do unwitting complementary reflections and divergences.

To honor the multiplicity of penned voices and forms, and to keep the associations they evoke open, this book is organized in sequence rather than defined clusters and chapters. Essays are stitched together and unfolded into a continuous stream of thought, at times connecting themes, and at others simply juxtaposing them to expose how the responses naturally or disruptively flow into one another.

Counting eighty-four entries from authors around the world, these essays conjure up an *exquisite corpse* of the state of our collective existence—and its translation into space. They constitute a collaborative attempt to critically and meaningfully engage with the issues threatening and upholding our ability to live together past, present, and future.

They range from ruminations about the political, social, and spatial contracts that undergird our mutual dependencies, to calls for greater recognition of historically othered modes of being and representation in and of the world. And from ety mologically and lyrically questioning the cultural and communal relevance of architectural elements—the tent, the threshold,

9

the wall, the bed—to highlighting architecture's radical potential as much as its complacency in forging governing systems, whether historically commendable or perilously global.

Several of the essays also provide very concrete case studies from the past hundred years as well as more recent examples of experimental reclaiming of communal rights, whether in the house, in the city, in schools, or at museums. Others offer a more focused and critical lens on the tools made available by the discipline and beyond to build reparations in post-disaster and systemic injustice contexts. And others still reflect on the limitations of human might and the expansions necessary to question the architectural subject and decentralize the power structures that govern both the field of architecture and the societies that it reinforces.

Freed from the burden of predominantly visual representation, the contributors to this book have, nevertheless, held on to the role that architecture could play in representing and embodying a collective life. Beyond architecture being their subject matter, and in their insightful brevity, they succinctly capture the indebtedness of our language to spatial cognition. They also powerfully convey the emotive role of the spaces they are delineating as they unfold from one scale of association and togetherness, to another: from empathy to love, affinity, curiosity, humanity, life and more.

RESPONSES TO
HOW WILL WE LIVE TOGETHER?

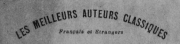

LES MEILLEURS AUTEURS CLASSIQUES
Français et Etrangers

J.-J. ROUSSEAU

DU

CONTRAT SOCIAL

ou Principes du Droit politique

Lettre à M. D'ALEMBERT sur les Spectacles

ERNEST FLAMMARION, ÉDITEUR
26, RUE RACINE, PARIS

CONTRACTS—SOCIAL, SPATIAL, POLITICAL

les engagera-t-il sans se nuire et sans négliger les soins qu'il se doit ? Cette difficulté, ramenée à mon sujet, peut s'énoncer en ces termes :

« Trouver une forme d'association qui défende et protège de toute la force commune la personne et les biens de chaque associé, et par laquelle chacun, s'unissant à tous, n'obéisse pourtant qu'à lui-même, et reste aussi libre qu'auparavant ». Tel est le problème fondamental dont le contrat social donne la solution.

Les clauses de ce contrat sont tellement déterminées par la nature de l'acte, que la moindre modification les rendrait vaines et de nul effet; en sorte que, bien qu'elles n'aient peut-être jamais été formellement énoncées, elles sont partout les mêmes, partout tacitement admises et reconnues, jusqu'à ce que, le pacte social étant violé, chacun rentre alors dans ses premiers droits, et reprenne sa liberté naturelle, en perdant la liberté conventionnelle pour laquelle il y renonça.

Ces clauses, bien entendues, se réduisent toutes à une seule : savoir, l'aliénation totale de chaque associé avec tous ses droits à toute la communauté; car, premièrement, chacun se donnant tout entier, la condition est égale pour tous; et la condition étant égale pour tous, nul n'a intérêt de la rendre onéreuse aux autres.

De plus, l'aliénation se faisant sans réserve, l'union est aussi parfaite qu'elle peut l'être, et nul associé n'a plus rien à réclamer; car, s'il restait quelques droits aux particuliers, comme il n'y aurait aucun supérieur commun qui pût prononcer entre eux et le public, chacun, étant en quelque point son propre juge, prétendrait bientôt l'être en tous; l'état de nature subsisterait, et l'association deviendrait nécessairement tyrannique ou vaine.

Enfin, chacun se donnant à tous ne se donne à per-

Inevitably, the allusion made in the initial program of the 17th International Architecture Exhibition of La Biennale di Venezia to a "new spatial contract" leads by association to the most important political statement of the Enlightenment: Jean-Jacques Rousseau's *On the Social Contract; or, Principles of Political Law*, published in 1762 in Amsterdam. This book was one of the sources of the French Revolution, and continued to be read until the twentieth century, for instance by Le Corbusier, who saw in it some guiding principles in his search for a supreme "authority," which could have endorsed his projects, as indicated by his scribbles in the margins of a copy of Rousseau's book he acquired in 1929.

One of the main principles proposed by the Swiss philosopher was to require the individual to forfeit his/her "natural rights," in order to gain the rights offered by citizenship, in a political system in which a legitimate administrative body would become the source of all decisions. This centralized pattern was obviously irresistible to those skeptical of democracy, such as Le Corbusier and many modernist designers.

But is it possible to translate this sound principle into architecture? One could consider that building without concern for the direct effects of a structure on its environment is a "natural right" of property owners. An obvious example could be found in the long shadow cast by today's super-thin New York skyscrapers on the neighboring blocks, or in the selfish pursuit of building programs in suburban areas without the least concern for the landscape generated—true to the "fuck context" attitude detected by Rem Koolhaas several years ago.

At the scale of the city, the race- or class-motivated reluctance of residents in upscale neighborhoods to see affordable housing or social infrastructure be built "in their backyard," or the rejection by other wealthy social groups of mass transit schemes in favor of automobile-centered mobility, seem also to be considered as "natural rights."

Following the theory of Rousseau—who pleaded for the replacement of isolated individual decisions by a sovereign institution, distinct from government, representing the general will—a new form of legislation could appear, in the preparation of which architectural, urban, and spatial issues at large would become themes of public discussion.

But in order for this discussion to fully take into consideration the expectations of those marginalized or affected by the politics or policies of selfish exclusion, elected officials and activists cannot be left alone. Experts knowledgeable about the concrete implications of these harmful actions and capable of formulating alternatives (not only in terms of form, but also in terms of legal provisions) have to be mobilized.

The issue is less to resurrect the generous but forgotten figure of the "advocacy planner" of the 1960s, than to expect from architects, engineers, landscape designers, and all those capable of foreseeing the long-term effects of development or building decisions, to be as engaged socially as they are in their professional production: not as demiurges, but as citizens aware of their ability to conclude a new, just contract.

Trained as an architect and an historian, Jean-Louis Cohen holds the Sheldon H. Solow Chair in the History of Architecture at New York University's Institute of Fine Arts. He has published more than forty books, including: *Building a New New World* (2020), *Le Corbusier: An Atlas of Modern Landscapes* (2013), *Architecture in Uniform* (2011), *Casablanca* (2002), and *Le Corbusier and the Mystique of the USSR* (1992).

Jean-Jacques Rousseau, *Le Contrat social ou principes du droit politique*. Paris: Flammarion, 1929. Copy owned by Le Corbusier.

SPECIES-
LIVING

How do we live *together* in the age of (global neoliberal) capitalism, whose ideology is linked to the evolutionary model of the struggle for survival? Or, if the naturalization of capitalism is no more than ideological fallacy, could there be a truly natural social order? A century ago, when the downfall of capitalism seemed closer than ever, philosophers and architects turned to nature to learn how to live together—to live as species. Guided by instinct, animals, they discovered, often demonstrate altruism and collectivity, for example, the maternal instinct or the equally instinctual organization of birds into flock formations. However, as Russian philosopher Alexander Bogdanov argued, unlike animals, the human collective is engaged in collaborative, constructive work directed towards a common goal. As an art of visualizing and reifying ideals, architecture, therefore, acquired an important social mission: as Marx had famously remarked, unlike bees and spiders, an architect "raises his structure in imagination before he erects it in reality." The most notoriously "utopian" Russian revolutionary projects, such as Nikolay Ladovsky's sketches for the "communal house" or Vladimir Tatlin's Monument to the Third International (both from 1919) were not utopias (fruitless dreaming) but projective architecture—representations of the social ideal that was to guide people's collective life and work. Indeed, as a wooden model that was paraded through the streets during mass gatherings and celebrations, Tatlin's tower found material existence independent of its fate as a building.

Unlike the individualized mass media of the second half of the century, such projects consolidated individuals, reminding them of their shared interests and of the necessity of comradeship in striving for them—they returned people from the unnatural, monadic existence to their biological essence of species-being, in which they willingly share their agency with others. Although this model of collectivity united people regardless of their gender, race, nation, or class, it is not unproblematic. From the vantage point of today, it is clear that it was hostile to independent judgement; that it universalized European culture; that it separated *homo sapiens* from other species and from the planet itself, which it treated as a mere resource for human utilization; and that its ethos of productivism justified the exploitation of labor. But can we dismiss goal-setting under the current predicament of crisis, in which only planning and coordination on a global level can allow planetary survival? What if we are not to reject but to decolonize projective thinking? Could architecture become projective without being authoritarian, utopian, Eurocentric, imperial, or manipulative (in other words, without becoming teleological in the negative sense of this word)? How could architecture express without monumentalizing, communicate without proselytizing, and unite without forging exclusiveness? The projective architecture of today does not look for creative solutions—the magic stick of neoliberalism, which deifies and isolates the individual—and instead seeks collaboration with scientists, policy-makers, and activists. Sharing agency and mitigating individual expression, this revolutionary architecture projects *together*, calling for a future in which we do not struggle but cooperate for survival.

Alla Vronskaya is the Professor of Architectural History at Kassel University, Germany. She holds a PhD from Massachusetts Institute of Technology. Her forthcoming book, *Architecture of Life: Soviet Interwar Modernism and the Human Sciences,* supported by membership at the Institute for Advanced Study in Princeton, NJ, explores intersections between architecture, labor management, and human sciences in modern Russia.

Nikolay Ladovsky, *Architectural Phenomenon of the Communal House,* 1920.

MAYBE WE ALREADY ALREADY KNOW HOW TO DO IT

FUTURE STEPLE

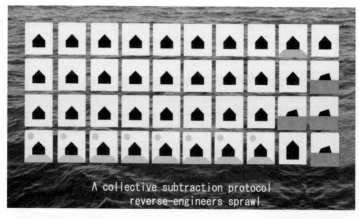

A collective subtraction protocol
reverse-engineers sprawl.

The same protocol can be used against wildfire risk.

The ticking time bombs of whiteness, inequality, and climate cataclysm make it ever more clear that the modern Enlightenment mind—with its myth of singular enemies and redemptive new solutions—is pretty useless.

There are no equations of certainty, but rather an opportunity to foster interdependencies. A more robust response may be a messy mix of many factors in physical space. Even the simple protocol for fighting pandemic—involving distancing, hand-washing, and face covering—is a lumpy mixture of human and nonhuman factors operating from the scale of microns to the scale of territories. And given the events of this past year, a broader culture now more clearly sees space as an instrument of violence, injustice, and lethality as well as repair, innovation, and survival.

The pandemic protocol is only the most obvious example of a form of innovation that culture routinely fails to comprehend. It may not be a quantitative expression, vaccine, or new technology that is most sophisticated, but rather the quality of the relationships between people, technologies, and ideas.

A protocol of interplay is an organ of innovation. It is not a solution. Problems are not eliminated but rather recombined to leaven and catalyze each other. It is different from designing a single object or building. It is a verb rather than a noun. It is a time-released response to changing conditions and political maneuvers. It is not expressed only in the anointed digital or econometric languages. Instead, it mixes heavy physical spatial information with digital, quantitative, econometric expressions as well as social and cultural evidence of all kinds.

Designing is entangling, and designing forms of interplay rewires and retunes that entanglement. Maybe what is needed is not a more precise measurement or data visualization of global dilemmas but rather a synthetic design imagination for manipulating them. Beyond pandemic, protocols for interplay can address, among many other things, migration, policing, gentrification, cooperative land tenure, automation, coastal retreat, reforestation, and compounding reparations.

At the heart of interplay design is mutualism—the resourceful recombination and matchmaking between needs and spatial assets. The mutualism that has long been central to abolitionist thought also often identifies a commons of values and relationships that are alternative to dominant powers and markets.

Interplay might also serve an expanded activist spectrum. To be together is to fight, even riot, for environmental, racial, and economic justice. But there is also work to be done to dull binary divides that authoritarian superbugs perennially weaponize and to reduce potentials for structural violence in organizations of all kinds. Often undeclared, spatial interplay might offer a tool for work to outwit the superbugs. It will never be done, and it will always go wrong, but maybe we already know how to do it.

Keller Easterling is a designer, writer, and professor at Yale University. Her books include, *Medium Design* (Verso, 2021), *Extrastatecraft: The Power of Infrastructure Space* (Verso, 2014), *Subtraction* (Sternberg, 2014), *Enduring Innocence: Global Architecture and its Political Masquerades* (MIT, 2005) and *Organization Space: Landscapes, Highways and Houses in America* (MIT, 1999).

KELLER EASTERLING

A protocol of interplay for reverse engineering sprawl in the face of flood or wildfire leverages collective risk to counter precarity.

LIVING TOGETHER IN HARMONY BY BALANCING THE QUADRUPLE BOTTOM LINE: FINANCIAL, ECOLOGICAL, SOCIAL AND CULTURAL PRIORITIES

Two-thirds of the world's population will be living in cities or other urban centers by 2050.[1] Meanwhile, by 2045, the United States will transition to a majority non-white population.[2] The racial and cultural disharmony present in the US today will only be exacerbated as density increases, if our society does not proactively design for harmony. We often confront financial, ecological, and social issues in our design processes, but we also need to prioritize cultural cohesion as our communities across the globe head towards an increasingly more diverse and complex future. I will discuss how balanced and thoughtful leadership, solutions-oriented creativity, and inclusive collaboration can help us live together more fruitfully, drawing upon stories of exemplary design that facilitates health and harmony in communities.

When I was a college student, I developed a concept called SEED, which grew to become what is now known as the SEED Network. SEED is an acronym for Social, Economic, Environmental Design and the SEED mission is to advance the right of every person to live in a socially, economically, and environmentally healthy community. Through this work early in my career and my more recent experience as a city government professional in Detroit, Michigan, national president of the National Organization of Minority Architects (NOMA) and principal at HOK, I can attest to the importance of cross-sector collaboration in solving our society's most pressing problems.

Leveraging the perspectives and resources of public, private, and not-for-profit entities is critical to creating more equitable communities that foster a sense of belonging for all. Our cities have a responsibility to establish policies that help their most vulnerable citizens have access to opportunities and vital resources. Not-for-profit organizations have a duty to fulfill their mission and support their constituents in ways that are more necessary than ever before in history. Corporations are increasingly being expected to create value for their client base while also demonstrating corporate social responsibility to help solve larger issues beyond their traditional roles.

As we embark on a new decade, we are witnessing advancements in technology bring the world together in ways we have never seen before. The sharing of information has bridged many divides, but it has also brought heightened awareness to disparities and injustices. The harmony that we wish to see in the world can be possible if our leaders prioritize humanity and the equitable balance of our collective financial, ecological, social, and cultural needs. When we are able to see the issues plaguing other humans and understand that our own humanity is interconnected, we can begin to understand our own sense of duty to lead effective change from our own positions of power and authority. Only when those who have power see that their strength is realized when empowering others will we experience the harmony in our world that transcends boundaries of all kinds. Design has the power to bring people together, once they discover and decide that being together is the best option that we have to thrive.

Kimberly Dowdell, AIA, NOMA, LEED AP BD+C, is a Principal at HOK in Chicago. She was the 2019–2020 National Organization of Minority Architects (NOMA) president. She is an award-winning architect, speaker, writer, and advisor.

KIMBERLY DOWDELL

1   "Population Division: World Urbanization Prospects 2018," United Nations, accessed January 25, 2020, https://population.un.org /wup/Country-Profiles.
2   William H. Frey, "The US Will Become 'Minority White' in 2045, Census Projects," Brookings, March 14, 2018, https://www .brookings.edu/blog/the-avenue/2018/03/14 /the-us-will-become-minority-white-in-2045 -census-projects.

Hope in Desolation, NOMA Service Project in Detroit, 2012.

THE AGE OF THE ACTIVIST ARCHITECT

CRAIG WILKINS

As I have written before, space is life; access to its benefits is the wellspring from which all else flows. Yet it is clear when considering the built environment that some communities are being left out of the conversation for just and equitable spaces. In the creation of supportive and sustainable design, many are being deliberately ignored. But what if things were different? What if architects worked to provide services to those traditionally left outside their target clientele? The other 90%? A careful examination of Hip Hop can provide some unexpected answers to this question.

Born out of the marginalized communities of the Bronx in New York City who refused to believe their lives were environmentally predetermined, Hip Hop—whose primary elements include rapping, b-boy-ing, graffitiing, dj-ing, and self-knowledge—emerged as a way for marginalized people to connect, rejoice, and simply affirm their existence. Derived from a need to be validated, Hip Hop has empowered the previously expendable. What was once seen as a small group of city-bound youth's act of desperation is now a borderless global phenomenon. It has made the dispensable indispensable. Today, one can find Hip Hop in such disparate places as Japan, Brazil, Denmark, Chile, Uganda, Cuba, Venezuela, South Korea, and Germany, to name a few.

Why is this important? Everywhere there is someone, some group, that is marginalized, alienated. Hip Hop speaks to and through them about a shared condition. By validating each member's existence, solidifying a group identity, raising collective awareness and entrepreneurial spirit to, finally, calling for political action, Hip Hop has in fact created a collective way of being with its own language, rules of belonging and behavior, values, material production, rituals, and institutions. This is commonly referred to as a culture. And every culture creates products that embody its particular worldview: music, literature, art, politics, and eventually, architecture. We've seen this evolution before. An early-twentieth century desire to create a classless society brought us Constructivism; a mid-century attempt at a universal society brought us Modernism; a late-century proposition of a decentered society brought us Deconstructivism. The current effort to facilitate a just and equitable society brings us to Hip Hopism.

Architects, like the early pioneers of Hip Hop, are presently faced with the problems of dispensable space, disposable buildings, and disadvantaged people. Understanding how mostly ignored youth from neglected environments with little access to capital and resources—material or otherwise—built a global, billion-dollar enterprise should provide invaluable insights, if not a direct blueprint, for resource-strapped architects who wish to work in distressed communities to help create empowering environments. If architecture is to remain viable as a profession, it will have to shed its traditional patronage model and evolve into an activist practice, communicating and demonstrating why design matters to everyone, always, and in all ways. One of the driving forces of the twenty-first century will be extending design beyond merely the creation of objects of desire into the areas of economic, social, and environmental justice. Hip Hop architecture, perhaps more than any other method of architectural production, is both noun and verb, both process and product. It moves the term "architecture" away from referring to the visual aesthetics of buildings alone to include their visible ethics as well.

R.I.P gentleman architect. The age of the activist architect has begun.

Architect, author, academic, activist, Dr. Craig L. Wilkins is a 2020 American Landscape Association Bradford Williams Medal recipient and 2017 Smithsonian Cooper-Hewitt Design Museum National Design Award winner. He is currently creative director of the Wilkins Project, a social justice, strategic design alliance that provides architectural, urban design and planning services, public interest design solutions, and expertise in engaged public discourse.

CRAIG WILKINS

Clockwise from left:
Typical urban condition in the twenty-first century: Abandoned factory in the middle of a Johannesburg residential neighborhood.

Something from Waste:
Community artists and architects build public seating for bus riders from discarded metal and doors from demolished houses in Detroit.

Typical urban condition in the twenty-first century: Building abandoned for three years before demolition, Detroit's East Side.

FOR A
FUGITIVE
TOGETHER

What is at stake in posing the question *"how will we live together?"* today? Indeed, has not the problem this question poses long been solved by the larger structures that continue to construct our present? If living together means the making common of infra-structural provisions and networks of dependency; the implementation of common political, legal, and social norms, and the accommodation of scales of togetherness they mediate; and the cultivation of a broadly shared horizon of expectation, then the past two centuries of liberal capitalism have done wonders never before seen to bring the world under a single imaginary of "living together."

Thus, I want to approach a different notion of living together through the work of a collective whose practices might help architects to recenter our creative focus from solutions for perceived problems to the collective imaginaries that work to frame them. In this sense, we can situate the notion of "living together" as a process of design rather than its end goal.

Organized in 2004, the activist group, Not An Alternative, has been building an insurgent form of activism intent on exposing how collective imaginaries are constituted and naturalized in institutions. As centers that concentrate collective power, institutions, they write, "are sites of struggle over who and what counts, over the ways we see and understand our collective being together."[1] Working between art, political activism, and design, their practices shift the site of struggle from aesthetic production (think institutional critique) to institutions themselves. Institutions, they observe, are "complex multiplicities, split within themselves and between themselves and their settings"—as such, they are ripe for creative forms of activism.[2]

Projects like The Natural History Museum (NHM) practice a form of activism that mobilizes the power of institutions directly. Conceived as an insurgent museum, the NHM's work ranges from exhibition programming to a pop-up museum bus to mobilizations within professional associations of museum workers. By participating as a certified institution, the group gains access to institutional space and leverages its legitimacy, through which it can build alliances and assemble counter-discourses of natural history from within. As they write, "[t]he Museum inquires into what we see, how we see, and what remains excluded from our seeing. It invites visitors to take the perspective of museum anthropologists attuned to the social and political forces inseparable from the natural world."[3]

By exposing nature as something constructed and mediated by institutions, the NHM makes public a different view of nature as both a common and contested category. In this space, the NHM is able to work an infrastructure through which struggles waged against extractive industries narrate a natural history of our present, while also opening up the museum as a living site for the construction of a common future.[4]

When we invoke "living together," we should insist that any future imaginary is first and foremost a political imaginary. Not "living together," but finding sites where "together" becomes political: choke points in the circulation and production of dominant cultural, social and epistemological norms also double as fugitive infrastructures in which counter imaginaries for new forms of living together can be collectively built.

Ross Exo Adams is Assistant Professor and Co-Director of Architecture at Bard College. He is the author of *Circulation and Urbanization* (Sage, 2019) and writes and lectures widely on the intersections of architecture and urbanism with geography and environmental humanities.

1   Not An Alternative, "Institutional Liberation," *e-flux journal* 77 (November 2016), accessed January 3, 2020, https://www.e-flux.com/journal/77/76215/institutional-liberation/.
2   Ibid.
3   "Mission Statement," The Natural History Museum, accessed January 4, 2020, http://thenaturalhistorymuseum.org/about/.
4   See, for example, the traveling exhibition *Whale People: Protectors of the Sea* that shows how killer whales are at the center of the struggle fought by the Lummi Nation for climate justice in the Pacific Northwest. "Whale People: Protectors of the Sea," The Natural History Museum, accessed January 6, 2020, http://thenatural historymuseum.org/events/whale-people -protectors-of-the-sea/.

A delegation of Indigenous leaders and allied museum workers at the opening of *Kwel' Hoy: We Draw the Line*, an exhibition by The House of Tears Carvers of the Lummi Nation and The Natural History Museum, Carnegie Museum of Natural History, Pittsburgh, PA, 2017. Coinciding with the 2017 ICOM NATHIST conference on the Anthropocene, this exhibition was one part of a cross-country tour, evolving museum exhibition and series of public programs uplifting Indigenous-led efforts to protect water, land and our collective future.

The Natural History Museum, *Expedition Bus*, 2014. 15-passenger bus on site at the People's Climate March, New York, September 21, 2014.

"WE WANT
BREAD,
KNOWLEDGE,
AND
THEATER"

A picture taken in late October 2019 in the abandoned Grand Theater in Downtown Beirut triggered in me the idea for this short reflection. Behind a jubilant Lebanese soprano, Monà Hallab, the phrase "We Want Bread, Knowledge, and Theater" was sprayed on a dusty, exposed concrete slab. I don't know whether this photo was staged or not, but I saw the slogan as a genuine *cri de coeur* emanating from the collective voice of an embattled generation of Arab youth who have been relentlessly agitating against their intransigent, corrupt, and oppressive rulers for the last decade.

The demand for bread or material sustenance is understandable in a foundering economy that has condemned huge segments of its youth to poverty and permanent unemployment. So is the plea for knowledge in a region that still suffers from woefully inadequate educational systems, hopelessly regressive and totally detached from our highly technological age. But asking for theater is a peculiar and somewhat unexpected request. In my opinion, it encapsulates an entire facet of living together that has been mostly damagingly absent from the realities of several generations of Arabs (and other youth of the poor South). This missing dimension is public space.

By public space, I don't only mean open urban areas like plazas, marketplaces, or shopping malls where people congregate, often while going about their own business. I mean spaces where people meaningfully engage in collective action, like learning, worshipping, celebrating, or protesting—hence my understanding of the demand in the Beiruti graffiti as an evocation of the theater as a public space.

The Greeks, who invented theater, understood it as part of an entire series of cultural activities involving all citizens that ranged from ritualistic festivals to political assemblies in the agora. These events were meant to underscore the participation of the citizen in the public life of the city. In this scheme, theater was both a planned spectacle and a space for dialogue. It was also the stage upon which an emotive kind of learning unfolded through the plays and their performance, the space, atmosphere, and setting, and the interaction between the actors and the audience, which was expected to be both scripted and freely participatory.

This interpretation of theater, admittedly a bit historicist, is how I read the slogan's demand. In the age of widespread protests of mostly disenfranchised youth worried about leaving their future in the hands of rapacious political and financial classes, theater, broadly conceived, provides an optimal public space of solidarity, expression, and exchange.

From this perspective, many spaces in the city can fulfill that spatial expectation with a healthy dose of freedom and minimal design intervention. Plazas and squares obviously can and have often functioned as temporary theaters, with corners occupied by speakers, dreamers, doomsayers, musicians, and all sorts of performers interacting with the passersby. Cafés, bars, and restaurants can become theaters, and many do, sometimes on a regular basis. And of course actual theaters can transcend the role of mere entertainment without relinquishing it as an instrument of their appeal, as the youth of Beirut hoped their neglected Grand Theater can become again what it once was.

What is needed to reclaim the "public" in these public spaces is the reaffirmation of a robust political commitment to the notion of the citizen as a trusted free agent in a collective whole that provides both respect and protection.

Nasser Rabbat is the Aga Khan Professor and the Director of the Aga Khan Program for Islamic Architecture at MIT. His interests include Islamic architecture, urban history, Arab history, contemporary Arab art, heritage studies, and postcolonial criticism. He has published numerous articles and several books on topics ranging from Mamluk architecture, to Antique Syria, to urbicide.

NASSER RABBAT

Marie-Rose Osta, Two still images of the Beirut Grand Theater, 2019.

TOGETHER
IN MOTION

SARAH MINEKO ICHIOKA

Part of living together is moving together. I have to get from A to B, you have to get from B to C, they have to get from C to A; en route our paths may cross or overlap. Multiply this by an urban population in the millions and the braiding of journeys becomes intricate. Get it right and the results can feel miraculous; human ingenuity and coexistence at their best.

Singapore joins other postindustrial East Asian and Eastern European countries as amongst the highest demand markets for mass transit, with over seven million daily journeys by bus, rail ,or light rail.[1] Government-led actions since the 1970s to invest in safe, extensive, and affordable shared transport have been coupled with efforts to inhibit use of the private car through road pricing, parking fees, and car licensing restrictions.[2] As of 2018, annual allowable car growth is 0%.[3] A small portion of the population may be housebound or chauffeured, but the majority of us living here—approaching 70% of modal share at peak hours—will, by necessity and by choice, use shared transport.[4]

In Singapore, spaces of shared transit are, alongside the country's public green spaces, amongst the primary places of coexistence for people from the widest possible range of backgrounds. On any given morning the MRT will carry canoodling young professionals, jet-lagged backpackers, and teenage boys in their National Service uniforms. On any given evening, the bus will carry a Filipina nanny chaperoning a child to ballet class, bargain-hunting senior citizens, and exhausted Bangladeshi construction workers heading home for dinner.

In a time when our virtual domains can seem insulated and antagonistic, the spaces of public transport offer small but humanity-affirming rituals of mutual accommodation and connection. The train and bus are spaces of equal standing, literally. Or more accurately, spaces where certain social hierarchies override others: we will give up our seat to someone much older, much younger, or visibly less able to stand than we are, regardless of class or race. Making space for those entering or exiting a crowded train, pointing out to your neighbor that he has dropped his ticket, playing peek-a-boo with the baby across the aisle; daily occasions to say to a stranger *Excuse me, Thank you, You're welcome.*

In a capitalist culture that overvalues efficiency and productivity, I appreciate that there's not that much to *do* on a train or bus aside from being with ourselves, with others, passing through the city. Yes, there are overbearing advertisements inside some central stations, and many of us are hypnotized by our smartphones, but once we're in motion the main view is our fellow passengers and the scenery outside the windows—vantages into the lives of others at close and further range, and reminders of the many possible ways of being in the world.

To be sure, public transport is no panacea for society's problems. I will never forget the San Francisco commuter train, when the man slouched in front of me injected into his scarred hand at the height of rush hour, surrounded by nonplussed commuters; the London metro where I turned to see a pickpocket grin as he pulled his hand out of my purse; or the Manhattan subway where I *hoped* the prone, blanket wrapped figure sprawled on the floor was only sleeping. Even in relatively orderly Singapore, train station entrances are a key location where destitute elderly or people with disabilities sell individual packets of tissues, a slightly more dignified, socially accepted form of begging. Places aren't truly public if they only accommodate certain kinds of people or show us only what makes us comfortable.

Yet Singapore's public transport system offers one of many promising examples where the future we collectively need—characterized by more sharing of resources and fewer planet heating emissions—can, with positive interventions, create conditions that are desirable for most of us in terms of individual human experience. Successful spaces of shared transport are well-connected, spacious, comfortable, easy to navigate, robust, even beautiful. Architecture and allied professions can do much to bridge the gaps between the necessity and desirability of these spaces of collective mobility.

Sarah Mineko Ichioka, Hon FRIBA, leads Desire Lines, a strategic consultancy for environmental, cultural and social-impact organizations and initiatives. She is a co-curator of *To Gather: The Architecture of Relationships*, the Singapore Pavilion at the 17th International Architecture Exhibition, La Biennale di Venezia, and the co-author, with Michael Pawlyn, of *Flourish: Design Paradigms for Our Planetary Emergency* (Triarchy Press, 2021).

1   "Mode of Transport," Singapore Department of Statistics, Singapore Government, last modified 2019, https://www.singstat.gov.sg/find-data/search -by-theme/population/mode-of-transport /visualising-data.
2   Yii Der Lew and Chik Cheong Choi, "Overview of Singapore's Land Transport Development 1965– 2015," in *50 Years of Transportation in Singapore: Achievements and Challenges*, ed. Tien Fang Fwa (Singapore: World Scientific Publishing, 2016), 6–10.
3   National Environment Agency and Land Transport Authority, "Vehicular Emissions Scheme to Be Extended by One Year to 31 December 2020," October 30, 2019.
4   "Transport," National Climate Change Secretariat, Strategy Group, Prime Minister's Office, last modified 2017, https://www.nccs.gov.sg/climate-change-and -singapore/reducing-emissions/transport.

Passengers on the East-West Line, part of Singapore's Mass Rapid Transit network.

ARRIVAL AND WELCOME

Johannesburg, South Africa's gold rush city, is a city of arrival. This large and fast-growing urban region is a place that people continue to migrate to in search of gold and a better life than the one they left behind. With its 53% migrant population, Johannesburg remains a city in flux.

As an urbanist I am aware of the economic impacts of built infrastructure, but I am more interested in what comes before that infrastructure. Efforts to address inequality through infra-structure projects only succeed if the ideals of equality are embedded in their design. It is for this reason that I have spent a significant portion of the past decade on a project I initiated to rescript Park Station—Johannesburg's major transport hub and arguably the largest transport node in sub-Saharan Africa.

Park Station is a building that is rich with meaning, heritage, identity formation, and design. These multiple layers allow for different interpretations by the diverse travelers who walk through it. The original Park Station building was an image of parallel and entirely separate spaces. It was designed by white people for white people, to be glamorous, generous, and exclusive. For black Africans, however, the same building is a symbol of servitude and humiliation.

The collective memory of the old station has largely been lost. Those familiar with the mothballed concourse are no longer. These days, few even know it exists. But I believe it can be an incredible place: activated by thoughtful programming and behaving like a truly public space that's about people coming together and feeling comfortable together. Park Station can be a place for trading and learning, symbolism and performance. A place to gather, to pause from constant movement. A place to just be urban. Architecture can become the conduit for this cohesion to happen.

In South Africa, we are so used to public spaces being contested that we feel we cannot just "be" in them. In 2011 I proposed to the city authorities and leading architects and academics in Johannesburg a rescripting of the old station: from a colonial place of exclusive travel to a meaningful meeting point for all. My vision for Park Station is to shift its exclusivity to inclusivity; to create a democratic arena that embraces the every-day connections of the station to the African continent and diaspora. To mark a grand arrival and welcome to all those visiting and moving to Johannesburg. To make of it a safe, warm, culturally rich passage through the city. The programmatic brief for the project envisages a variety of activities to improve the day and nightlife of the precinct, including an African market of goods and services; performance spaces; nodes of learning; and a retail offering, including a continental canteen.

This is a moment to consider how architecture, which was used to separate South Africa, can now be used to bring people together. People should have the right to make the city in their image—especially in a fledgling post-Apartheid democracy still finding its place in the world. The people must draft the proposals! The government should act as facilitators—not as lazy dispensers of creativity-killing tender documents, designed around price and not, well, design. Administrators should buy ideas and concepts from citizens who are passionate about city-making. Those not from the city are welcome, too, forming teams that are multidisciplinary and transnational. In this way the urban environment becomes a canvas for expressions and sharing—a piece in the global gallery.

Zahira Asmal is an urbanist and director of The City, a research, publishing, and placemaking agency she founded in 2010. Her work addresses inequality and democracy making. Zahira published three books that examine socioeconomic, political, spatial, and cultural environments shaping South Africa's big cities and currently serves on the board of advisors for the International Archive of Women in Architecture.

Exploring Joburg through Addis, 2015.

1932 Park Station, 2014.

Welcome to Johannesburg, Park Station, 2019.

LINGER,
FOR A MOMENT,
IN THE CITY

SARA M. WHITING

Our world is evermore urban. It is time for the way we live to catch up. That means slowing down.

In 2016, the European Commission's *Atlas of the Human Planet* assessed the globe to be 85% urban, understanding the term to include not only urban centers, with populations of 50,000 or more at densities of 1500 people/km^2, but also all urban clusters, with populations of 5,000 and densities of 300 people/km^2.[1] One can quibble over metrics (by the UN's count, the world is 55% urban), but the simple fact is that the world's population is coming closer together and, in doing so, is constructing relations that are at once more dense and less self-similar.[2] Nothing could be more exhilarating than the heterogeneous density of our cities. But are we living urban lives?

The internet, like television before it, brought the world into our homes. It has also neatly sorted us into benign, and sometimes not so benign, interest groups. People flock to websites that are invariably mirrors, connecting us with people just like us. Even as we live cheek by jowl, our public realm has become similarly parsed, which is to say, self-absorbed. Technology has eliminated waiting and, along with those now missing pauses, the chance encounters that might come from our moments of collective loitering.[3] We don't go to conference rooms, grocery stores, libraries, or post offices. Our agendas, vegetables, novels, and stamps come to us. When we do go out, technology ensures that we don't waste any time getting lost. What would Shakespeare or Walt Whitman or Wes Anderson have done without the chance encounters born of errant time?

While one can criticize the Greek agora, the seventeenth-century New England town meeting, the eighteenth-century French salon, or the twentieth-century global suburban mall as not being truly public (none of these examples were open to anyone and everyone), our shared, even if somewhat drifting, public realm has always nourished our appetite for discourse, for the ideas and actions upon which we found our day-to-day lives. Being public means having exchanges with people we bump into, people who are not like us but have everything to do with who we might be tomorrow. In a world comprised solely of accumulation, without unpredictable exchange, are we really a public?

If waiting has become elusive, we can design pauses. Designing wayward time yields potential contemporary agoras.

The chaotic exuberance of our growing density offers extraordinary opportunities to render urbanity public in its very gaps and uncertainties. Opportunities lie between our front doors and the street, in lobbies, and between floors; they lie along streets and in the entrances to parks. Rather than succumb to the homogeneous efficiencies of Otis, Schindler, and JCDecaux, design can produce prospects for an ornery notion of exchange. Not coolly efficient. Certainly not theatrically self-promoting. Contemporary public life might better be understood as a kind of discursive cigarette—without smoke or nicotine, but with plenty of metaphorical fire—over which one can linger while sharing the exotic air of so much new and intense urban life.

Sarah Whiting has been Dean and Josep Lluís Sert Professor of Architecture at the Harvard University Graduate School of Design since 2019. She is also a design principal and co-founder, along with Ron Witte, of WW Architecture, based in Cambridge, MA. Previously, Whiting served as the Dean of Rice University's School of Architecture from 2010 to 2019.

SARAH M. WHITING

1   Martino Pesaresi, Michele Melchiorri, Alice Siragusa, and Kemper Thomas, eds. *Atlas of the Human Planet: Mapping Human Presence on Earth with the Global Human Settlement Layer* (Luxembourg: Publications Office of the European Union, 2016), 41.

2   United Nations, Department of Economic and Social Affairs, Population Division, "World Urbanization Prospects: The 2018 Revision. Key Facts" (New York: United Nations, 2018), 2.

3   Ginia Bellafante "What We Lose by Hiring Someone to Pick up Our Avocados for Us," *New York Times*, January 31, 2020, http://www.nytimes.com/2020/01/31/nyregion/what-we-lose-by-hiring-someone-to-pick-up-our-avocados-for-us.html?searchResultPsition=1.

Ginza, Tokyo, Japan, 2019.

EPICENTER

We live together in different forms: when seismic forces shake our common grounds, our being together gravitates in relation to an epicenter. Such has been the situation in Santiago, Chile, as of October 18, 2019. A transport fare increase occasioned massive fare evasions; repression ensued, and in no time, protests erupted. In a few days, over a million people crowded Plaza Baquedano claiming basic rights and *dignity* (not *money*, as analysts would have expected). It is not that money was absent as a concern, but *dignity*—a more profound yearning—triggered people's desires for decency, empathy, and equality, as well as their expectations about being together in peace. Since then, Plaza Baquedano has become our emotional, political, and actual epicenter.

The plaza is one of those "squares" (more like a glorified roundabout) where radiating avenues converge. Situated by the edge of the colonial grid, its esplanade is vast enough to expose the massive barrier of the Andes—a telluric reminder of our insular condition. Plaza Baquedano is most effective as the actual and symbolic frontier between the districts occupied by the distinctive strata that articulate our very unequal society; a sort of ground zero, often reclaimed by football fans when celebrating a victory. It is where urban tribes converge when demonstrating, for they know that in that spot they gain massive exposure. In the fifties, a lone photographer armed with a tripod attracted provincial visitors looking for their portrait to be registered against the equestrian figure. Eastward and upstream, the natural and social gradients merge, leading towards *barrio alto*, the upper crust districts.

Camillo Sitte would have derided Plaza Baquedano for its spatial looseness, its formal ineffectiveness, and the erroneous emplacement of the equestrian statue of local hero—army commander Manuel Jose Baquedano—right in the middle, usurping a unique emplacement from which to contemplate the landscape. Although elemental, the composition brings geometry, topography, and topology together.

In a simple diagram Aldo van Eyck illustrated how a topographic inflection determined "two ways of being together." Its concave form fashioned a crater where all sightlines converged, as in stadia, whereas its convex one determined a mound with all sightlines diverging towards the horizon; land-forms determined the modes of being together and their corresponding levels of reciprocity. Plaza Baquedano makes a very shallow mound. The sculptural group comprises a soldier and a victory figure flanking opposite sides of the plinth, and above it the general on his horse, facing west towards downtown, the seat of power: the composition is thoroughly conventional. As if following a wild carnival, the ensemble is now covered under thick layers of paint and drapes. Hundreds of messages scripted over the plinth relay so many claims, whilst saturating its sober elements with color. Massive rallies bring people together: roaring, climbing the effigy and waving flags in an anonymous promiscuity that charges the polis with the intense feel of common- ality embedded in the expression *we, the people*.[1]

Rodrigo Pérez de Arce is a practicing architect. He has taught at the AA, University of Bath, University of Pennsylvania, Cornell, and Harvard GSD amongst others. He presently holds a professorship at the Catholic University, Santiago. His topics of interest include historical, landscape and programmatic dimensions of public space. He has published on topics of landscape, public space, and play.

Susana Hidalgo, *Re-evolución*. 2019. Seized by the multitude, as portrayed in Susana Hidalgo's "Re-evolution," the equestrian sculpture becomes in itself a plinth for the people and their emblems. Eighteen months later, with the sculpture removed, the site stands idle and decentered, awaiting the next mass gathering.

1   This text was written around October 2019, at the time of massive popular upheaval in Chile. The onset of the COVID-19 pandemic thereafter disabled public gatherings, and as a result, the square stands mostly empty, nowadays, with sporadic gatherings that have caused the monument to be repainted to match its original condition after successive layers of graffiti, until March 2021 when due to attempts to topple it, the equestrian sculpture was removed. However, the events described in this essay have changed the political landscape in the country and will no doubt dictate the ways in which Chileans define their future ways of "being together" in our new constitution.

CAN WE COEXIST WITH OIL? THE BAMENO WAORANI BELIEVE THEY CANNOT

On July 16, 2019, a Baihuaeri Waorani delegation led by Penti Baihua, President of OME Yasuní, and the renowned environmental and human rights lawyer Judith Kimerling, came to Quito to demand that oil companies remain outside the borders of the Tagaeri Taromenane Intangible Zone (with the Spanish acronym, ZITT), its Buffer Zone, and ideally, the Yasuní National Park. The ZITT was created in 1999 through a presidential decree to protect indigenous peoples in voluntary isolation. It clearly stated that this area would remain off-limits to all forms of extraction, an exceptional condition considering that the Ecuadorian state has reserved rights over subsoils almost everywhere else—including underneath national parks and communal territories, with future concessions in mind. Even though the perimeter of the ZITT was outlined by oil interests that were oblivious to the occupation and movement patterns of semi-nomadic groups, it has been relatively successful at preventing the encroachment of oil blocks. On May 21, 2019, the current president of Ecuador, Lenín Moreno, a socialist turned IMF champion, added an "exception to the [extraction] prohibition" for infrastructures such as "perforation and exploitation of hydrocarbon platforms." His addendum triggered the outrage of Waorani and other indigenous groups, as well as of environmentalists. In a 2018 popular referendum, 67.31% of Ecuadorians voted yes in response to the question: "Do you agree with enlarging the ZITT by at least 50,000 hectares, and reducing the oil exploitation area authorized by the National Assembly in the Yasuní National Park from 1,030 to 300 hectares?" Indigenous groups in Amazonia have borne the bulk of negative social and environmental externalities associated with oil extraction. It is not surprising that the Waorani, who would be adversely and directly affected by Moreno's exception, mobilized on multiple fronts that received ample attention from the international press. In the specific case of the Baihuaeri, their discomfort is expressed beyond the juncture of Moreno's presidential decree 751 and his attempt to open up the ZITT to oil infrastructure.

For the Baihuaeri, as for countless indigenous and Afro-descendent groups in the Americas, the core question remains land tenure. Without a secure claim to their territory, the Waorani fear they will continue to be displaced and dispossessed, as they have been since the Texaco-Gulf consortium found commercial reserves of oil in 1967. The concern of the Baihuaeri has intensified since Rafael Correa's government, without due process of prior and transparent consultation, transferred property rights from discrete Waorani groups to NAWE (Waorani Nationality of Ecuador), whose elected director must be approved by the state. The Baihuaeri have responded to this last threat to their livelihood with the proposal "*Deje Vivir* (Let Live)." The irony of Ecuador right now is that it has shifted from the effusive "*Buen Vivir*" of a socialist government that reduced and misused the ancestral Kichwa concept of good living or *Sumak Kawsay*, to the demand "*Deje Vivir*" of a Waorani group from whose perspective neither socialism nor neoliberalism has delivered it from the ominous pressures of extractivism, let alone improved their well-being (what they had before contact). "We want to live without money, without oil, without contamination. We want to live the Waorani way of life,"[1] says Penti Baihua. May this Biennale resonate with the radical stance of the Baihuaeri, ask the hard questions, and provide the soft answers: the forest is the future; oil, a pending past.

Ana María Durán Calisto is a doctoral candidate at UCLA where she works on the history of urbanization in the Amazon basin, with a focus on the oil urbanisms of Ecuador. She co-founded Estudio A0 with Jazz Kalirai in Quito. She has taught at multiple schools including FADA-PUCE, Columbia University, and Yale School of Architecture, among others. She has co-edited *Beyond Petropolis: Designing a Practical Utopia in Nueva Loja* (Oscar Riera Ojeda, 2015) and *Urbanismo ecológico en América Latina* (Editorial Gustavo Gili, 2019).

1 Money is a relatively new presence in Bameno. The Waorani today need money to cover for several expenses. When Penti said this to me, he was probably reminiscing the days in which his community was fully autonomous and self-sustaining. Currently, the Baihuari run a community-based ecotourism project in order to make ends meet.

Baihuaeri Waorani of the Yasuni resist oil extraction.

47

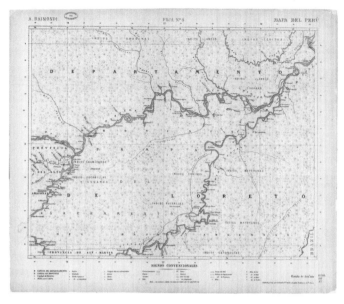

CARTOGRAPHIES OF THE FOREST

MARIA ALEJANDRA LINARES TRELLES

"Muitwatsu, a boa, is the mother of the cochas (lagoons). When she moves her head, water trembles... if she leaves, large muyunas (whirlpools) form...The second Sun—Wepe Mukuika—is where the fish, the lizards, the dolphins, the paiches, and the small boas live. Here also lives Ipira mama, master of the water, who controls the river fluctuations..." [1]

Indigenous communities like the Kukama Kukamiria, who inhabit the forest in what is today the Peruvian Amazon, describe through oral tradition a universe composed of interconnected worlds, where human and other-than-human subjects interact reproducing forms of sociality and conviviality. Captured in artifacts, narrations, and visual representations, these counter-cartographies provide alternative forms of knowing, relating, and living together.

Peru, like many other regions in the Global South, had its territory reconfigured under the lens of capitalist extraction. Since the sixteenth century, the accelerated need for natural resources has fragmented the world into extractive zones. These regions support "economic growth" and "development" elsewhere, while their inhabitants, primarily indigenous populations, remain in a state of precarity, fighting to defend and preserve their ancestral territories, subsistence, health, culture, and lifestyle.

In his 1897 "Map of Peru," naturalist Antonio Raimondi reduced the Amazon forest to an unstructured, emptied space represented in green hatch. [2] Although he recognized the presence of indigenous populations, he disregarded their agency in the transformation of the forest. For him, the fact that indigenous peoples had not yet exploited the resources of the region was not seen as a result of a cultural modality, but as a failure of intellect. By contrast, he elevated the presence and achievements of "industrious Europeans," promoting settler colonialism, agricultural, and mining estates, as well as infrastructure for commerce. [3] Extractivism, tied to racial capitalism, still operates through maps. Their imposition of a detached "view from above" homogenizes territories under the perceived reality of those in power while flattening the complex dimensions of ground-level dynamics, including community interactions, values, and ways of living. These maps circulate through different spheres, reproducing and maintaining discourses of *terra nullius* enabling the disappearance of human and other-than-human communities.

In contrast, indigenous knowledge—represented in "indigenous counter-cartographies"—understands the land not as surface to be occupied or exploited but as an active agent in a larger integrated ecosystem, in which what happens in one area affects another. These spatial representations shift perception, playing with the section view over the top view to reveal a complex space shaped by a profound awareness of ecological systems and care dynamics. Facing the urgent need of a new spatial contract, and acknowledging the power of visualization in our current moment, indigenous images of sovereignty and habitation challenge disciplinary knowledge, informing shifts in the ways we see, navigate, and know territories. Furthermore, they have the potential to transform landscapes, and imagine alternative forms of living together, in which the common "we" includes humans and other-than-humans, thus recognizing the sets of relationships that connect both. Amidst crises that threaten life at a planetary scale, what futures can be found through indigenous counter-mapping and spaces of resistance?

Maria Alejandra Linares Trelles is an architect from Lima, Peru. She works across design, research, writing, and curation to explore architecture from a sociopolitical perspective, focusing on issues around landscape, ecology, and justice. She holds a degree in Architecture from Pontificia Universidad Católica del Perú, and a Master of Science in Critical, Curatorial, and Conceptual Practices in Architecture from Columbia University's GSAPP.

1 This extract explains part of the Kukama Kukamiria cosmology by natives Witurio Yuyarima Chota and Wilfredo Pereyra. Cited in Fernando Santos Granero et al., eds., *El Ojo Verde: cosmosvisiones amazónicas* (Lima: Programa de Formación de Maestros Bilingües, AIDESEP, Fundación Telefónica, 2000), 58. Translation mine.

2 Consisting of 32 sheets, Antonio Raimondi's "Map of Peru" was printed and published in Paris by the Erhard Frères between 1887 and 1897. The map is considered the synthesis of his work and the first detailed map of the Republic of Peru, after its independence from Spain in 1821.

3 Antonio Raimondi, "Viaje de Lima a Tarma, Chanchamayo, Vitoc, Moyobamba, Uchubamba, Jauja," The Diary of Antonio Raimondi, no. 3, 1855, 34–66, Archivo General de la Nación, Lima, Peru.

Sheet No.8 of the "Map of Peru" by Antonio Raimondi, 1887–1897.

Drawing of Kukama Kukamiria Cosmology by native artist Miguel Augusto Caritimari.

A FRAMEWORK IRRETRIEVABLE?

The question of coexistence is of perennial importance. Humanity, after all, thrives as an interconnected fabric. The architect's role in stewarding a new "spatial contract" to contribute to this collective flourishing is thus a needed reminder of our place in the world. Yet, the notion that architecture—as a singular means of building practice—could effectively address wider sociopolitical rifts or environmental degradation is increasingly moot. With inequity and destruction caused by megalomania and the fragmentation of values, it is perhaps more meaningful to contemplate how the architectural enterprise could nurture values cognizant of diverse expressions of coexistence. *Such an inclination, perhaps, should not preclude the reality of human endeavors as less invincible or accountable to larger socio-environmental interdependencies, even those governed by a spiritual authority.* A personal reflection on such modes of coexistence has recently, and fortuitously, taken shape for me around the Hindu-Balinese concept of *tri hita karana* ("three causes of well-being"), which I encountered consecutively through rather divergent means: first through the recontextualization of Stephen Lansing's study of the Balinese *subak* system at the Sharjah Architecture Triennial, and then through visits to a housing compound in the village of Keliki and the Lempuyang Temple in Bali.

This concept of maintaining an equilibrium in the tripartite relationship between overlapping and interdependent forces— the relationship between humans (*pawongan*), between humans and the spiritual realm (*parhyangan*), and between humans and the natural environment (*palemahan*)—has been central in the ordering of daily socio-religious rituals and spatial-spiritual orientations in Bali. These three dimensions play out intimately in the system of *subaks*, or the network of irrigation associations. Based on the belief of water as a gift, decisions on water allocations and the timing of water supply are made by consensus among *subak* members, believed to be the stewards in the management of this gift, and supported by rituals mediated by water temple priests. Such a practice demonstrates the interdependency between religious, spiritual, and cultural practices and cooperative resource management of the ecology of rice terraces.

In the realm of the built environment, *tri hita karana* implies that direction becomes a determining factor in physical, cultural, religious, and social "space." The siting, layout, and proportion of a housing compound or a temple are aligned with the *kaja-kelod* (sacred-profane) conception of cosmic structure that forms an interlocking set of horizontal and vertical orientations in which man becomes a tiny part, yet also a microcosm, of the universe. Such pursuit of balance and propriety in the relationships between the occupant, the building, the natural environment, and the cosmos is seen in the design of the Lempuyang Temple. As a *pura puseh*—a temple directed towards the mountain—it was built to make the east node of Bali be in equilibrium with other cardinal points of the island, and oriented such that its *candi bentar* (split gate), through which one enters the temple's outer court, perfectly frames the peak of Mount Agung—the island's tallest mountain and spiritual reference of *kaja* (sacred).

These examples of how the built environment is bound to the ceremonial and cosmological may seem like an unrecoverable reality in our pervasively secularized societies. Yet, they serve as probes to consider how a purely techno-scientific, economic, and progressive mode of comprehending humanity falls short of representing its fullness. They raise the possibility of exercising architecture through a set of grammatical components in reverence for systemic vulnerabilities and potentials of well-being across multiple realms. The shifting factors of a self-willed and market-driven novelty and inventiveness need not, then, be the sole criteria of merit.

Shirley Surya is Curator of Design and Architecture at M+, the new museum for visual culture in Hong Kong. She contributed to building the M+ Collections through her research on plural modernities in greater China and Southeast Asia. At M+, she co-curated exhibitions including *In Search of Southeast Asia through the M+ Collections* (2018) and *Building M+: The Museum and Architecture Collection* (2014).

Pura Penataran Agung Lempuyang, Karangasem, Bali, Indonesia, December 2019.

POSTS AND
PEOPLE

HUSSA SAH AL-SALEM AL-SABAH

How could we live together? How would we benefit from it? What are we trying to accomplish by living together? Is it better resource management in the construction and maintenance of physical structures? Is it the elimination of individual isolation? Is it the creation of/return to active communities where the impact on the group is an important component of decision-making?

In his article "The Future of Architecture Is in Tents," noted critic and writer David Huber suggests the answer to these questions is tents. "Tents are shelter for the vulnerable and displaced—migrants, refugees, homeless persons—and support for tons of cultural and religious activities: sporting events, music festivals, benefit galas, wedding ceremonies, awards shows, after parties, spiritual pilgrimages.... [T]emporary marquees are the framework of a growing number of modern rituals, the shape of otherwise formless and ephemeral congregations."[1]

In my region, I can't help but think of our tents, created by the first architects: women. Women planned the space and wove the sides and roof of the tent, while men sourced the poles and erected the structure.

Traditional tent-based communities, regardless of where they existed in the past, shared characteristics we value today. The elements of the tent—the fabric and the posts—were designed to allow flexibility in scale and mobility. As people joined the communities, whether through familial growth, geopolitical movement, or just through happenstance, tents could be enlarged and new tents could be added. The materials were reused and recycled until they ultimately became fuel for the fires providing heat and sustenance.

With thousands of people inhabiting a vertible tent town, cooperation was imperative to the success of the group. Hunting, cooking, child-rearing, entertaining, packing, and moving were among the community activities, executed in common spaces wherein all shared responsibilities. In fact, the tent itself was often a shelter for sleeping, with life happening both inside and outside its walls.

The early-sixth-century CE chieftan and poet, Al-Afwah al-Awdī, wrote a poem that begins with the line: "Among us are those that have not built anything great for their people." The poem "Daliah" continues:

55

A tent cannot be built without posts, and the posts are worthless
if they are not strongly embedded in the ground,
And if you have these posts,
and they are embedded deep into the ground,
and you have good people living in the tent,
then things will be good.

So, while I am not advocating that we move into tents, I am suggesting we consider the wisdom that emerged from the culture. Clearly the poet was referencing much more than a tent; even fifteen hundred years ago, he knew that it wasn't the structure that made the tent a home and a group of tents a community, but the quality of the people living in them.

Hussa Sabah al-Salem al-Sabah is the director general of the Dar al-Athar al-Islamiyyah (DAI) and co-owner of The al-Sabah Collection, one of the largest and most comprehensive private art collections in the world. She serves on the Metropolitan Museum of Art (NY) and The Museum of Fine Arts, Houston (TX) Boards of Trustees, among others.

HUSSA SABAH AL-SALEM AL-SABAH

Illustrated folio depicting the "Preparation for the Flight of Iraj from his Camp," from a manuscript narrating the exploits of Amir Hamza (the uncle of the Prophet Mohammad), known as the *Dastan-e Amir Hamza* or *Hamzanama*, commissioned by the Mughal emperor Akbar, India, third quarter of the 16th century. Ink, colors, and gold on cotton, 68.2 × 53 cm.

1   David Huber, "The Future of Architecture Is in Tents," *Garage*, October 23, 2017, https://garage.vice.com/en_us/article/8x5nyz /contemporary-architecture-tents.

THRESHOLDS

Certainly, border and threshold are mutually dependent concepts. One cannot think of a border without simultaneously imagining its potential to be crossed, and no more can a threshold be investigated without considering its dividing function. Nonetheless the two terms do not concur. Anthropologist Arnold van Gennep appositely defined the difference between border and threshold in his 1909 work *The Rites of Passage*. At the border, van Gennep asserted, a "particular space" is demarcated by the ritual placement of "border stones or borderlines" and thereby made inaccessible to outsiders. In contrast to the border, the zone comprises a neutral area between delimitations and is manifest at the territorial level as well as in its urban correlations: in the village, town, district, temple, or house. Thereby steadily decreasing in scale and degree of publicity, he continued, the zone reduces itself from a landscape space such as a desert, swamp, or jungle, through single architectural elements such as the gate in the wall, the portal to a district, or the door of a house, to the individual tectonic structural elements such as the simple stone, beam, or threshold. According to van Gennep the threshold is not divisive but connective; it is not bound to a border experience but rather is destined to overcome it.

More than anywhere, it is at the threshold that the architectural imaginary of a time leaves its traces. It is at the threshold that its manifold conditions find their expression: in the revolving door, the inclusionary and exclusionary mechanisms of the modern metropolis; in an elevator, the negotiation of inner and outer space within a multi-storey building; in slatted blinds a variable mode of dealing with the issue of representation; in the body scanner, the ever more prevalent mapping of the human body as electronic data; in the waste disposal unit, the different means to treat waste within and outside a building; in mirrored facades, images of public space; in the barcode, consumer behaviour and monitoring; in the telephone, the medial networking of individuals; and in lines marked on the floors, the only answer to today's viral threat. Such narratives, which serve to structure and organize space, have been made manifest in the numerous innovations that complement the traditional doorway. The threshold attests to this.

This is generally viewed and the more today—in norms, laws, politics (but also academia)—as the only way to be modern. What remains however ignored in the process is that it could also open up previously unknown potentials, where architecture is no longer

understood as a series of new, sometimes invisible, borders
between the interior and the exterior, the private and public, the
safe and the unsafe, the clean and the dirty, the accessible and the non-accessible, but is instead conceived as the possibility to design a multiple transitional space—a *mi-lieu*—between different areas, separated and variously articulated via constructive, social, infrastructural, and other layers, which instead of braking down these various relationships differentiate them.

Laurent Stalder is an architectural historian at ETH Zurich. The main focus of his research and publications is the history and theory of architecture where it intersects with the history of technology. His latest publications include *Architecture/ Machine* (gta Papers 1, 2017), and *Architectural Ethnography* (Toto Publishing, 2018).

LAURENT STALDER

Still image from the film *Manolete*, directed by Menno Meyjes, with Penélope Cruz and Adrien Brody, UK/Spain, 2007.

THE
ARCHITECT
DECIDES

DIDIER MAEITVRE

The practical and financial outlay of architectural projects makes them especially liable to reflect the uses and values of their time as interpreted by patrons, sponsors, and public commissioners. This has been the case since the first column of the Acropolis went up, or that of the Hagia Sophia, the Chartres Cathedral, El Escorial, or the Chrysler Building. Starting with the rise of the administrative state in the seventeenth century, architectural projects of great magnitude have been for the most part, if not directly, the brain-children (or at least the adoptive children and wards) of government officials—economists, politicians, and technocrats. And from the seventeenth to the nineteenth century, the technocratic worldview shapes public architecture, first in the guise of the great administrative palaces (Versailles, Whitehall, the Winter Palace) that swept aside urban anarchy, then through the open vistas of a rationalized body politic (The Raj's reinvented Delhi, Haussmann's new Paris, Victor Emmanuel's dream of new Rome, Bismarck's Großstadt Berlin, etc.). This vision has grown apace in the twentieth century. The administrative state triumphant is the message of inter-bellum Fascist architecture, as it is the message of postbellum Corbusian-style public works, the purest and most notorious enactment of which is Brasília. Not only is architecture the expression of those in the position to commission it, it is the expression of a topdown vision of society by those few who have seen the New Jerusalem and aim to take the rest of us there. It may be regrettable from a liberal standpoint but there it is: architecture moulds lives, creates a *modus vivendi*, and gives rise to patterns of civic compliance.

Nowadays, the vision of much of the ruling class in the Western world is no longer imperialistic, nationalistic, or hyper-rationalistic; it is all about horizontal channels of communication, connectivity, mobility, migration, inclusivity, and diversity knitting us together into global cosmopolitanism. It is a vision of uprooted individuals drawn from every imaginable walk of life crossing paths and mingling and living together, both mindful of and cordial with their differences. As in the past, architects are called upon to implement this new dream of the body politic. It is a noble dream, this vision of all the people getting along while ceding nothing of what makes them different. Yet it is a planned dream nonetheless, not an emergent one that springs from the actions of people on the ground. We seem to stand before a contradiction. The ethics of

61

diversity should entail letting people decide how to live their own lives and how much they are interested in their neighbours, then letting their architectural surroundings grow out of these personal decisions. However, the politics of diversity nudge and superintend these choices through environment planning which engineers people to behave in a desirable fashion (in this instance, to be diverse and inclusive and connected). This touches on the paradox of modern architecture. While it operates in a society that upholds democratic freedom, architecture (at least the kind that originates in blueprints) constrains freedom. It necessarily builds walls. Whether transparent or not, those walls lead us to foregone outcome. In the end, of course, human beings vote with their feet, and the imp of daily use, improvisation, and ingenuity takes over the plan.

Didier Maleuvre is Professor of Comparative Literature at the University of California, Santa Barbara. He has written several books on literature, art, and the history of ideas, among which more recently, *The Art of Civilization: A Bourgeois History* (Palgrave Macmillan, 2016) and *The Legends of the Modern: A Reappraisal of Modernity from Shakespeare to the Age of Duchamp* (Bloomsbury, 2020).

DIDIER MALEUVRE

World Trade Center Transportation Hub, New York, USA, 2019.

Entrance to a building, Udine, Italy, 2019.

TOWARDS A
TRANS-SPECIES
ARCHITECTURE

BEATRIZ COLOMINA & MARK WIGLEY

L'interno di un giardino d'inverno con piante esotiche ed un grande acquario a parete.

"*How will we live together?*" is the question but who or what is the "we"? "We" implies similarity, kinship. "Together" implies heterogeneity, as when different things are brought together. "Together" can never simply be "we." Living together means hospitality to the other. And living means also dying, however slowly—living with cancer, depression, anxiety, addiction, allergies—and conflict or doubt, things that architects are usually mute about with their endless narratives of instant happiness through design. To live together is to share the pain of others. A hospitable architecture could never be painless.

If it is we humans that need to learn to live together differently, then the call is for a new architecture of hospitality, of living with the other, taking the risk of the other, embracing a new we not formed by similarity but by difference, even the difference you don't recognize—the unclassifiable, shifting, multiple, contradictory, elusive, obscure, and uncertain. In other words, a hospitality to different kinds of difference.

This counters the contemporary politics so dominated by fear of the other—the sectarian insistence on walls, regulations, limits, barriers, nationalisms, and bubbles. Architecture is complicit in this endless drawing of lines. Most architecture is generated by fear. The idea of architecture is to keep things out: weather, people, animals, insects, dirt, noise, vibration.... Architecture is a form of editing, filtering, blocking, obscuring, or hiding. To contribute to new forms of hospitality, architecture must be turned against itself. It must embrace what it currently excludes. An architecture for living together might need to be an anti-architecture. Or at least an architecture that paradoxically offers shelter to its outside.

Humans are not so human after all. They are formed and constantly reformed by a cross-species collaboration with countless different types of microorganisms. The microbiome of tens of thousands of different species of bacteria that humans depend on means it is never clear where the human begins and ends. To care about the human is to care about extraordinarily dense, complex, and ever-shifting networks of exchange between countless different organisms. Anthropocentric architecture needs to give way to new forms of trans-species hospitality. The real clients of architecture are microorganisms: bacteria and viruses.

Insects, software routines, and weather patterns are also clients. Trans-species architecture must include all the fellow animals and plants, whose biodiversity humans steadily reduce, forgetting that the planet itself is a living creature, lived with rather than just lived in. Technology can't be excluded from the "we" either since there is nothing more human than technology—not just devices and infrastructure, but codes, programs, operating systems, networks, protocols, and algorithms.

For this expanded "we," much can be learned from designers and thinkers like Lina Bo Bardi, who developed a trans-species architecture tuned into plants, animals, and insects. Not by chance, she worked to undermine lines between popular and elite, indigenous and immigrant, north and south, human and non-human. A new architecture of trans-species hospitality also means to embrace those architects that expanded the concept of hospitality more radically than "we" could recognize at the time.

Beatriz Colomina is the Howard Crosby Butler Professor of the History of Architecture at Princeton University. Her latest book is *X-Ray Architecture* (Lars Muller, 2019). Mark Wigley is Professor of Architecture at Columbia University. His latest book is *Konrad Wachsmann's Television: Post-Architectural Transmissions* (Sternberg Press, 2020).

Lina Bo Bardi and Carlo Pagani, Illustration from the article Finêstre, *Lo Stile*, no. 10 (1941): 25.

Lina Bo Bardi, *São Paulo Museum of Art*, perspective drawing, 1957–68.

WALLS OF ASSOCIATION: PARADISE

HAMED KHOSRAVI

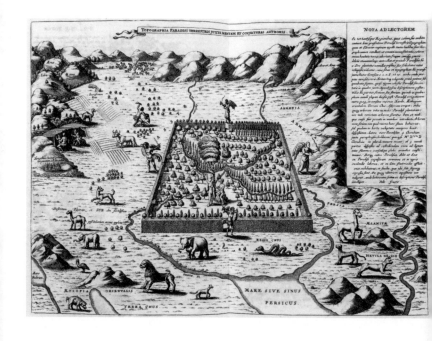

Of all the architectural elements, the wall comes first. The primary purpose of a wall is to establish a relationship. Association comes before separation.

Zoroastrian accounts characterize the universe as the opposition of two poles: the Wise Lord and the Evil Spirit. In this conflict, the very goal of mankind is to protect itself from evil forces. Such protection can only be secured through the intervention of a sovereign power who builds the most perfect earthly place, paradise—a breeding ground for people to reach the ultimate purpose of creation, which is happiness.

The Persian root of the word paradise (*pairi-daêzā*) nevertheless does not bear any image of a holy promised garden, as extensively promoted in the Abrahamic religious beliefs. Paradise literally means a "walled (enclosed) estate;" the word insists on the idea of the wall as the "divider of space" as it defines what does or does not belong to the protected context. The wall here is *not* a defensive wall; the old Persian word *daêzā* is rooted in a verb that means "to construct from the earth" or "to be made of clay." It divides and separates, and thus reproduces space and shapes a collective subject; it signifies and has the sense of a "dwelling place," "an earthen enclosure," or "to live in:" in other words, the city.[1]

The idea of the city, for the Persians, was firmly tied to the ultimate goal of creation, "happiness for mankind." The terrestrial paradise appears in the form of a frame of association, an organizational diagram that would establish dialectical relationships between power, inhabitants, and territory.[2] Such a frame goes beyond a model, figuration, or abstraction. It performs as a device to support a communal mode of inhabitation in harmonious exchange with the territory and with forms of power. Such performance produces a form of life that is irreducible to individuals and that addresses, instead, a collective subject. In this shift, architecture acquires a singular new role, quite different from the traditional notion of a closed system or architectonic—it becomes profoundly political. It measures, maps, and modulates the terrain through its projection of a certain state of association and power-relations onto the topography. Through framing the subjects such architecture becomes inherently collective—a form of sanctuary for almost any innovative collective action.

HAMED KHOSRAVI

Like all other memberships, citizenship requires a form of commitment—a binding contract that validates the performance of the civic subject to define the relationship between the individual, the territory, and the city. There is a new possibility for architecture to encompass such forms of life and to enable the idea of a political commitment. This form of living is projective association. It is neither a permanent contract nor the stable pleasure of final bliss. It is rather an active engagement in the present that enables the possibility of imminent change. Walls are spatial devices to establish and preserve such collective integrity, between human and non-human subjects, and the space they inhabit. Frames to recreate paradise on earth.

Hamed Khosravi is an architect, researcher, and educator. He received his PhD within 'The City as a Project' programme (Berlage Institute/TU Delft). Khosravi currently teaches at the Architectural Association School of Architecture, London. His research and projects focus on the relationship between architecture, territory, and politics of urban form.

Athanasius Kircher, *Terrestrial Paradise*, a rectangular frame enclosing the terrain with a crisp wall, 1675.

1   See my glossary entry, "Paradise," in *The City as Project*, July 4, 2011, http://thecityasaproject .org/2011/07/paradise.
2   Ibid.

ENTWINED;
SURROUNDED BY
BENEDICTIONS

Following another fitful night, she thanked me—again this morning—for making the bed.

Unmade or otherwise, the bed is a slate upon which dreams materialize. Beds efficacious and affective, it is in their contemplation that paradoxical complicities can be observed between the production of bodies at rest and the rest of bodies consumed by work.

Inhaling, I shield myself, overcome.

One of the 279 objects bequeathed to the Metropolitan Museum of Art in 1920 by the architect William Milne Grinnell is this enigmatic object depicting an amorous couple: upon a pillow, one lover wears a headdress, whilst the other appears to mount the first beneath striated bedding.[1] The figures smile, their pleasure enframed within the heavily-restored ochre band of cursive writing in which the Arabic words for "victor" and "perpetual glory" can still be read.[2]

I, too, sometimes contemplate my bed—our bed—as a battlefield.

Last summer, archaeologists successfully conducted analyses of anthropogenic layers within a cave. Their stratigraphy recovered the earliest evidence of deliberate bedding construction: two hundred thousand years ago, stratum of ash appear to have been purposely placed between those of aromatic grasses and woodier vegetation.[3] Paleoanthropologists hypothesize that the ash was meant to block the breathing and biting apparatuses of arthropods, leading to their dehydration and death. In this early bed of ash and medicinal plants, domination maintains a spectral presence. The bed already a place from which the rustling actions of human bodies attempt, and incessantly fail, to stabilize an unstable world they inhabit.

Crawling under covers, I am bound to utter promissory oaths into the darkness: tomorrow, another day.

Axis mundi, each bed, centers elsewhere. A vehicle for transcendence, the bed remains untamed despite pedantic tracking of its histories and the overwhelming profusion of age-old bedtime banal. How to avoid disenchantment between the sheets? My own bed resonates with vulnerability, delight, and repose. Fittingly, my partner and my son, too, claim this bed as their own. The bed, a stake and site of unrequited labor. Most tired, I exhale loudly, waking all around me with a start.

Khaled Malas is an architect and art historian from Damascus. He lives in New York City. His son, Walid, was born in the summer of 2019.

1   Measuring 16.2 × 11.1 × 4.1 cm, this object (accession number: 20.120.66) is manufactured from molded siliceous ware, glazed in opaque white, and luster-painted, perhaps with two colors. Attributed to twelve- or early thirteen-century Iran, its exact function and meaning remain debatable. A similar object, glazed in green, is currently at the Museum für Islamische Kunst in Berlin. Both may well have been made from the same mold. Scholars have speculated that the represented subject matter possibly belongs to medieval iconographies of festive intercourse and might have been exchanged as a nuptial gift. See the recent scholarship on so-called "Ceramic House Models": Maria Vittoria Fontana, "A New Understanding of the Seljuq Ceramic Models of Houses: A Review Article," *Annali Sezione Orientale* 79, no. 1-2 (2019): 306–315; Martina Rugiadi, "Model of a House with Amorous Couple," in Sheila Canby, Deniz Beyazit, Martina Rugiadi, and A.C.S. Peacock, *Court and Cosmos: The Great Age of the Seljuqs* (New York: The Metropolitan Museum of Art, 2016), 78–79; Alain F. George, "The Illustration of the Maqāmāt and the Shadow Play," *Muqarnas* 28 (2011): 1–42; Margaret S. Graves, "Ceramic House Models from Medieval Persia: Domestic Architecture and Concealed Activities," *Iran* 46 (2008): 227–251. For William Milne Grinnell, see Joseph Breck, "The William Milne Grinell Bequest," *Metropolitan Museum of Art Bulletin* 15 (1920): 273–275; "William Milne Grinnell, B.A. 1881," *Bulletin of Yale University: Obituary Record of Yale Graduates 1920-1921*, 17th ser., no. 22 (1921): 114–115.

2   Such benedictions are common on wares from this period and are perhaps reminiscent of repetitive phrases in song or prayer. In this case, the benedictions demonstrate the bed as a space for conquest. I too propose that this object is best experienced whilst singing. I suggest a rendition of Bob Dylan's "Leopard-Skin Pill-Box Hat," track 3 on side 2, *Blonde on Blonde*, Columbia Records, 1966.

3   The cave, known in the literature as the "Border Cave," is a rock shelter on the South African side of the border with Eswatini in the Lebombo Mountains. In addition to the vegetal remains, scientific analysis of the bedding also identified assemblages of lithics, fragments of bone, and rounded grains of ochre. Lyn Wadley et al. "Fire and Grass-Bedding Construction 200 Thousand Years Ago at Border Cave, South Africa," *Science* 369, no. 6505 (August 14, 2020): 863–866.

Molded, glazed, and luster-painted
siliceous ware depicting an
amorous couple.

THE BED
IN THE
DRILL HALL

Recent events testify to how ideas of community and their survival are constructed through the isolation of different bodies, segregated according to their productive, biological, and political conditions. We have recently seen, for instance, how ill individuals are isolated from the rest of the healthy population in armored public facilities repurposed as hospitals. Inside their large-span halls, ill bodies are distanced from each other in mathematically arranged spaces. Three meters apart from one another, these beds conform to a composition of endless grids, extending under industrial ceilings. Photos of these bed landscapes made the rounds online at the early onset of the pandemic, instantly evoking other historical images of pandemics, and inscribing them within a genealogy bridging disjointed periods of exceptionality. However, this act of isolating distinct individuals—an activity to which architecture actively contributes—is not episodic: it lies at the very core of current understandings of togetherness.

In 1981, a landmark decision by the New York State Supreme Court established that New York City "shall provide shelter and board to each homeless man who applies for it provided that… the man by reason to physical, mental or social dysfunction is in need of temporary shelter."[1] The legal, spatial conditions of this temporary shelter were defined as "a cut above the streets," signaling its difference from the rest of the population enjoying a stable home.[2] The bed constituted the key conceptual and material instrument around which the law defined the homeless shelter, interpellating the homeless individual as an arrested body. Once it was ruled that "the operator shall furnish each resident" with a bed, the statutes eschewed terms which referred in any way to the individuals themselves, leaving this piece of furniture to determine dimensions, materials, and spatial capacity. The homeless person was not only confined from the "functioning" rest of the community, but in her identification with the bed, her sheltering deemed her as inanimate, unproductive.

In 1983, to comply with the Supreme Court resolution, the City administration resorted to a series of New York State-owned properties to palliate the lack of space in municipal shelters. In January of the same year, while the Winter Antiques Show was being held in its drill hall, the Head House of the Park Avenue Armory facility in New York was furnished to receive a first batch of one hundred and fifty homeless men. In 1984, the municipality tried to increase the sheltering capacity of the building to a total of four hundred homeless men by placing some of them in the drill hall, conveniently separating their beds.[3] But this operation was discontinued due to pressures from nonprofit organizations supporting the homeless, as well as protests from the local community, which argued the incompatibility of the presence of homeless people with the artistic and cultural activities taking place in the building.[4] As a result, homeless individuals were restricted to the fourth and fifth floors, and their circulation throughout the building was segregated from that of cultural and art visitors.[5]

The logics of survival that today determine the isolation of ill bodies from healthy ones exacerbate and expose an intrinsic condition of how current societies function. As lawyer and urban planner Peter Marcuse observed in addressing the rise of homelessness in the US during the late 1980s, the isolation of the homeless subject was critical to the perpetuation of the neoliberal order that produces inequality. Having this body out of sight, in a space distinct from those of housed individuals, avoids people correlating political and economic measures with increasing poverty. Ultimately, their isolation averts a crisis of legitimacy in the current political system.[6] Addressing isolation's spatial mechanisms is thus key to determining how we will live together.

Lluís Alexandre Casanovas Blanco (Barcelona, 1985) is a New York and Madrid-based architect, curator, and scholar. He is the recipient of several awards such as the Bauwelt Prize 2019, the Simon Architecture Prize 2018, and the FAD Prize 2017. He has worked for institutions including the Oslo Architecture Triennale 2016 and the MNCARS Reina Sofía.

More than 30 members of the Kentucky Air National Guard's 123rd Civil Engineer Squadron set up hospital beds and clinical space at the Kentucky Fair and Exposition Center in Louisville, KY, April 14, 2020.

Photo by Don Hamerman included in Joe Klein, "The Homeless on Park Avenue," *New York Magazine*, April 16, 1984, 22.

1   Final Judgment by Consent, Callahan v. Carey, Index
    No. 42582/79 (Sup. Ct. N.Y. County Aug. 26, 1981).

2   Regarding how these standards were fixed, see my "A Cut
    Above the Streets: Robert M. Hayes, Co-Founder of Coalition
    for the Homeless, in Conversation with Lluís Alexandre
    Casanovas Blanco," *Ed Journal*, no. 2 (Spring 2018): 58–65.

3   Deirdre Carmody, "More Homeless to Go to Armory on
    Park Avenue: Hundreds to Be Housed at Enlarged Shelter,"
    New York Times, March 17, 1984, 27.

4   Reporting for *New York Magazine* in 1984, when the shelter had
    just been installed in the Park Avenue Armory, John Klein delved
    into the "rather strange sight of indigent men—some obviously
    mentally ill, some obviously alcoholic—wandering the same halls
    as socialites on their way to a private party in the officers' mess
    or Biedermeier dealers at the winter antiques show." More recent
    accounts have also stressed the shock that seeing these two
    populations at once produces. In an article penned by Nina
    Bernstein, for example, the Park Armory is identified as "the
    only place in New York where art patrons drinking Champagne
    share the elevator with homeless women on their way to their
    shelter." Similarly, Michael Shnayerson describes the building as
    a sort of melting pot mixing "well-dressed New Yorkers entering
    the Armory, students showing them to their seats as the night's
    contingent of 80 homeless women heads up to its renovated
    fourth-floor shelter." These statements read, at times, as cynical
    illusions of successful class intermixing. Klein, "The Homeless
    on Park Avenue," *New York Magazine*, April 16, 1984, 24;
    Nina Bernstein, "No More Shelter from the Storm; Renovation
    Will Evict Homeless Women from Armory," *New York Times*,
    April 11, 2001, B1; Michael Shnayerson, "The Fabulous (Second)
    Life of the Park Avenue Armory," *Departures*, April 22, 2014,
    https://www.departures.com/art-culture/culture-watch
    /fabulous-second-life-park-avenue-armory/.

5   While gallery-goers use the main door at Park Avenue, shelter
    users enter the building through one of the two old service
    entrances in the basement, located at 66th and 67th Street, a
    system at work to this day. When the Park Avenue Armory
    Conservancy was finally granted the stewardship of the Armory
    in 2006, the group appointed award-winning Swiss architects
    Herzog & de Meuron to conduct the necessary preservation
    operations in order to transform the building into a first-rate
    cultural facility. Although the architects were willing to refurbish
    the fourth and fifth floors corresponding to the shelter, the
    Conservancy allegedly refused. A member of the design team at
    Herzog & de Meuron, in discussion with the author, March 2018.

6   Peter Marcuse, "Neutralizing Homelessness," *Socialist Review*
    88, no. 1 (1988): 69–97.

CAMPING
TOGETHER

The historian Daniel T. Rodgers once referred memorably to the United States as a "disordered, violent camping expedition."[1] It is certainly possible to read the European settlement of the continent in these terms—the wanton despoliation and pollution of forests and wetlands, prairies and waterways, together with the human and nonhuman communities they supported, has been widely documented; and the temporary and flimsy nature of log palisades and sod cabins struck eighteenth-century visitors like Alexis de Tocqueville as forcefully as balloon frames and popcorn ceilings do travelers today.[2] The United States has always been a nation of mock-ups and false fronts—a storm surge of profit-driven water mills and mines, shantytowns and plaster "white cities" platted out via rapacious treaties and land rushes. The remarkable emptiness of the territory—its still-sparse settlement and thin, unconvincing sprawl—is the mark of a frontier mentality that couples "go west young man" with a fundamental lack of commitment to any place beyond immediate extraction of sustenance or gain. The result is a debris field akin to the casual litter-strewn sidelines of marathon routes—a million Dixie cups discarded half-full of Dasani, *en passant*.

Living as I do in the last strip of west before the West runs out, I can't help but couple Rodgers's comment with the aphorism attributed to Frank Lloyd Wright: "tip the world over on its side and everything loose will land in Los Angeles." "Loose" strikes me as the operable term here—at a loose end, loosed, lossy, lost. The crisis of the unhoused is inescapable in Los Angeles. Tents nestle in the dells of the city, punctuate medians, bloom along highways, begin to populate the parks. Skid Row is a row no longer, but a region, with its own de facto laws and codes. An advocate explains to me that a woman who lives across the street from my home had a baby on the sidewalk. I watch city workers in hazmat suits rake needles out of a red and grey half-dome tent sized for two sleeping bags. It strikes me that this is less a city under siege than a city left to its own loose, native urbanism—the urbanism of short-term avarice, long-term special interests, and NIMBYism that has always flourished in frontier towns. Even East Coast, colonial states like Massachusetts have failed to invest enough in their settlements to put telephone wires and electrical cables underground outside of the immediate urban core; California, the land of tinsel stage sets and gold rushes, is far behind. According to official

77

tallies there are over 60,000 homeless people in Los Angeles (the twelfth largest economy in the world); and more than 150,000 in the state as a whole (the fifth largest economy in the world). How should we live together here, in the midst of a nightmare holiday trip sustained by ludicrous inequities and indifference, and laid out in miserable encampments for all the world to see? Do not think the answer is only political, in the glad-handing, caucusing, promising stump speeches of local and national officials. Do not think the answer is only technological— cheaper, better, more innovative solutions to the problem of housing fellow humans. The answer is also, and probably most fundamentally, in our collective cultural imagination—in how we view our relationship to the places we inhabit and the communities that form around us. Architecture is concerned with that imagination. This is our role.

Marrikka Trotter, PhD, heads the History and Theory curriculum at SCI-Arc, where she has taught since 2017. Her current research examines the relationships between the historical exploitation of oil and water resources in Los Angeles and the city's urban form.

MARRIKKA TROTTER

Gelatin silver print of a shack on the edge of a private dump in Glendale, California, photographed on December 7, 1931, with typed caption, from *The Habitations of the Unemployed in Los Angeles County, 1931–1932* (Los Angeles: Los Angeles County Department of Health Services).

Gelatin silver print of a "Hoover Town" homeless encampment on 2nd Street in Los Angeles, photographed on February 4, 1932, with typed caption, from *The Habitations of the Unemployed in Los Angeles County, 1931–1932* (Los Angeles: Los Angeles County Department of Health Services).

1   Daniel T. Rodgers, *Atlantic Crossings: Social Politics in a Progressive Age* (Cambridge, MA: Harvard University Press, 1998), 42.
2   Alexis de Tocqueville, *Democracy in America*, trans. Henry Reeve, vol. 2, *The Social Influence of Democracy* (New York: J. & H.G. Langley, 1840), 53.

TO CHANGE SOCIETY BY CHANGING THE CITY: LESSONS FROM RED VIENNA AT 100

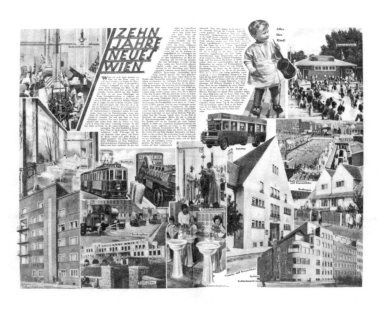

EVE BLAU

In 2019, Red Vienna—the radical program of municipal reforms that, between 1919–1934, reshaped the social and economic infrastructure of the Austrian capital along Social Democratic lines—turned 100. In Vienna, the anniversary was marked by a year-long engagement with the ideas, policies, and initiatives that drove the program. Vigorous debate about the program's successes and failures was carried out in the pages of *Falter* (Vienna's premier weekly news magazine known for its investigative reporting on politics, media, and culture), and in two exhibitions: *Das Rote Wien, 1919–1934. Ideen, Debatten, Praxis*, organized by the Wien Museum (and accompanied by a five-hundred-page catalogue) and *Das Rote Wien im Waschsalon Karl Marx Hof*, installed in the central monument of Red Vienna, the Karl Marx Hof.

Over the course of the year I was drawn into these public debates and the collective reflection they elicited. This gave me the opportunity to enter into a new dialogue with the City of Vienna and the urban architectural program of Red Vienna, which I had spent many years studying and writing about, and which I believe is one of the signal achievements of twentieth-century urban and social imagination. Today, it seems to me, the imagination that shaped the architecture of Red Vienna has renewed significance for our thinking about the city and the agency of architecture, particularly as we seek answers to the urgent question posed by La Biennale di Venezia's 17th International Architecture Exhibition: *How Will We Live Together?*

To begin, it is necessary to emphasize that while Red Vienna produced a vast amount of housing, it was not a housing program. Instead, it was a comprehensive urban project that set itself the task of making the city a more just and equitable environment for all members of society. The primary instrument of that project—in which the vital connection between social program and urban architectural form was forged in Red Vienna—was an ambitious building program that involved the construction of over four hundred buildings known as *Gemeindebauten* (municipal buildings), in which housing, social services, and cultural institutions were distributed throughout the city. By 1934, when Red Vienna succumbed to the reactionary forces that would soon overpower much of democratic Europe, more than two hundred thousand people (or, one-tenth of Vienna's population) had been rehoused, and the city provided with a vast new social welfare infrastructure.

It is important to remember that the *Gemeindebauten* were produced by a democratically elected municipal government, which took responsibility for the welfare of its citizens, treated them with dignity, and created social and spatial environments that gave them control over their lives.

Architecture and urban design played a key role in this project. It was the urban architectural design of Red Vienna that reclaimed private space in the city for public use and reconfigured the spaces of everyday life in ways that gave agency to their users, granting them the right not only to inhabit but also to shape their city and its future according to their own needs and desires.

Today, when the large-scale provision of public services including housing, education, and healthcare, is increasingly left to the market or to private companies operating on behalf of the state or other public bodies, we can learn a great deal from *re-reading* Red Vienna and its legacy very carefully. Not only did it spawn a remarkable housing program, it also embedded important, larger knowledge in the built fabric of Vienna about how cities can act on behalf of their citizens, how they can work to construct urban life around goals of social equity and public responsibility, and how—for those of us in the design disciplines—architectural intelligence can play a critical role in that effort.

Eve Blau is a professor at the Harvard University Graduate School of Design, where she is Director of Research. She has published widely on modern architecture and urbanism. Her books include *The Architecture of Red Vienna, 1919–1934/Rotes Wien: Architektur 1919–1934. Stadt-Raum-Politik* (MIT Press, 1999/Ambra, 2014), awarded the Victor Adler State Prize, 2015; *Baku: Oil and Urbanism* (Park Books, 2018) awarded 2019 DAM Architectural Book Award.

EVE BLAU

Karl Ehn Architect, Karl-Marx-Hof under construction, c. 1928.

"Ten Years of New Vienna," *Der Kuckuck*, May 19, 1929, 8–9.

ROOSEVELT ISLAND IN NEW YORK CITY: AN ANSWER FROM THE 1970S TO HOW WE CAN LIVE TOGETHER

LIZABETH COHEN

As relevant as the theme *How Will We Live Together?* is to the world today, with its rising economic inequality and ethnic and nationalist tensions, it is not a new question. Hence, it is instructive to revisit a time in the not-too-distant past when that question was asked—and answered—with concrete physical and social solutions. During the 1970s, the New York State Urban Development Corporation (UDC) transformed the semi-abandoned Welfare Island in the East River of New York City into a model "New Town in-Town," as it was called, and then renamed it Roosevelt Island.[1]

The UDC was created as a public benefit corporation in 1968 by Governor Nelson Rockefeller, with the reluctant approval of the New York State legislature, which feared the creation of a state agency as powerful as Rockefeller wanted this one to be. Because he was charging it with the tough challenge of building affordable housing and turning around the state's declining cities, he felt it would need extensive powers, such as the ability to override local zoning. As further insurance of success, Rockefeller recruited an experienced person to head the UDC, Edward J. Logue, with his proven track record for making things happen and attracting federal dollars in New Haven and Boston.

Logue had long been frustrated with the limitations of working at the municipal level to solve urban problems, particularly in addressing the limited supply of affordable housing available to low-income Americans and the racial and class residential segregation that seemed only to be growing with post-World War II suburbanization. So when given a statewide agency with vast powers and funding, Logue seized the opportunity to create an intentionally mixed-income, mixed-race community in the middle of New York City. Welfare Island's 147 acres had long housed institutions that the city wanted kept at a distance, such as prisons, insane asylums, and chronic disease hospitals. By the late 1960s, only two hospitals remained. Building upon a plan designed by prominent modernist architects Philip Johnson and then-partner John Burgee, Logue's UDC began developing a socially diverse, pedestrian-oriented, and environmentally and technologically innovative community. Major architects of the era—among them John Johansen, Louis Kahn, Gerard Kallmann and Michael McKinnell, and Josep Lluís Sert—were hired to design the island's structures. Not only were residences intended for diverse incomes and ages, but commitments were also made to house people with disabilities and to ensure that thirty percent of the population were minority. To maximize social mixing, day care centers and mini-schools were scattered throughout the various residential buildings.

Roosevelt Island opened to new residents in 1975. Sadly, however, the UDC's social ambitions contributed, along with the state's fiscal crisis, to the agency's collapse that same winter. Ed Logue's utopia would never be fully completed as planned, and market-rate housing has been added in recent years. But even today Roosevelt Island remains an unusually diverse part of New York City, a reminder of what social and financial commitment can make possible.

Lizabeth Cohen is the Howard Mumford Jones Professor in the History Department at Harvard University. She is the author most recently of *Saving America's Cities: Ed Logue and the Struggle to Renew Urban America in the Suburban Age.* Previous books include *Making a New Deal: Industrial Workers in Chicago, 1919–1939* (Cambridge University Press, 1990) and *A Consumers' Republic: The Politics of Mass Consumption in Postwar America* (Knopf, 2003).

Roosevelt Island, Ed Logue's Utopia in the East River of New York City. Roosevelt Island embodied Logue's idealistic goals for the UDC. The project aimed to mix residents along income and racial lines. It was also car-free and handicap accessible, long before the latter was common, and it used technology in innovative ways.

Combining Historic and Modern Structures on Roosevelt Island, early 1970s. Historic buildings were already on the island, like the Chapel of Good Shepherd here being repurposed as a meeting and interfaith facility. They were preserved and surrounded by modern apartment buildings of various sorts, ranging from subsidized rentals to market-rate cooperatives. The mix aimed at attracting residents of diverse incomes.

1   This essay draws from research published in Lizabeth Cohen, *Saving America's Cities: Ed Logue and the Struggle to Renew Urban America in the Suburban Age* (New York: Farrar, Straus & Giroux, 2019); see the book for more details and sources.

LIZABETH COHEN

"TOGETHER IN DISAGREEMENT"

FELICITY D. SCOTT

"*How will we live together?*" With difficulty, of course, and through a process of constant negotiation, disruption, and ongoing forms of refusal "to be governed thusly," as Foucault might say. Questions of cohabitation and forms of governance, which are questions of democracy, now have to be asked not just within the framework of nationhood and citizenship, but with respect to the operation of a global governing apparatus and its neoliberal disposition. Architecture forms part of any such governing apparatus, and its reflex to solve problems, invoke technocratic logics or economic ones, and be pragmatic, tends towards potentially dangerous political territory. This risk of closing down spaces for democratic negotiation was recognized in the mid-1970s by Professor of International Law, Richard A. Falk.

In the context of a conference dedicated to imagining new ways of living together in outer space—the Conference on Space Manufacturing Facilities (Space Colonies), which took place at Princeton University in May 1975—Falk refused the reduction of all aspects of life to economic and social scientific parameters and the management of bodies and psyches, with their well-being assured in physical terms; in other words, he resisted precisely the framework through which architectures for extreme environments are typically conceived, including those at play at the conference. In a lecture titled "New Options for Self-Government in Space Habitats," Falk embraced the prospect of space habitats (he refused the word colonies) as "restoring confidence in the future," reminding us that science and technology might contribute to the global good. He introduced a distinct set of concerns and procedures into the techno-scientific conversation, also challenging the framework of private enterprise, American vanguardism, and the trickle-down mentality by insisting on a different form of "global orientation." For the space colonization venture to be legitimate, he insisted, it required the inclusion, from the start, of non-American and particularly "Third World" voices in conception and planning, its terms expanded from those of the "experts." It would also have to guarantee a role for an international organization to manage geopolitical rivalries, which would remain, and shift from a proprietary model to "something that benefits the world as a whole."[1] After offering caveats on futurology, and refusing economic rationales and narratives of security that closed down such spaces for democratic negotiation, he underscored the need for mechanisms of global coordination that might function as frameworks for national diversity and human solidarity. My question, then, is how might architecture be reminded of the need to keep open such political spaces; how might the discipline and profession be reminded of their roles in forging the disposition of any such global governing apparatus; and how, in turn, might it operate to interrupt or re-inflect such systems of governance to more democratic ends? How, that is, can democracy take place in architecture?

Felicity D. Scott directs the PhD program in Architecture (History and Theory), and co-directs the program in Critical, Curatorial, and Conceptual Practices in Architecture (CCCP) at Columbia University's GSAPP. Her books include *Architecture or Techno-Utopia: Politics After Modernism* (MIT Press, 2007), *Ant Farm* (Actar, 2008), *Outlaw Territories: Environments of Insecurity/ Architectures of Counter Insurgency* (Zone Books, 2016), and *Disorientations: Bernard Rudofsky in the Empire of Signs* (Sternberg Press, 2016).

1   Richard A. Falk, "New Options for Self-Government in Space Habitats," in *Space Manufacturing Facilities (Space Colonies), Proceedings of the Princeton/AIAA/NASA Conference, May 7–9, 1975*, ed. Jerry Grey (New York: American Institute of Aeronautics and Astronautics, Inc., 1977), 181.

Rick Guidice, *Agricultural Modules in Cutaway View (multiple toroids)*, 1975.

Don Davis, *Construction Along the Torus Rim*, 1975.

LIFE AFTER EARTH: NADER KHALILI'S VISION FOR SUSTAINABLE MOON BASE OUTPOSTS

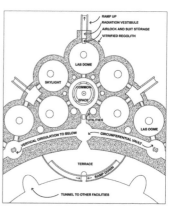

The confluence of several epochal events in the 1960s and early 1970s created the conditions which led scientists, engineers, and architects to lay down bold plans for collective living on lunar surfaces. These ambitious plans were set in motion by the Soviet Soyuz/Vostok and American Mercury, Gemini, and Apollo NASA missions, which commenced with the launch of the first human into space in 1961 and culminated in the landing of humans on the moon in 1969. Yet, as lavish as these government-supported space programs were, permanent lunar outposts would have required unfeasibly large expenditures as the US became embroiled in Vietnam and the oil crisis.

Indeed, whether backed up by scientific claims or by the pop culture of the Apollo era, the majority of ambitious plans for lunar settlements were economically unviable. It is against this backdrop that the ideas of the Iranian-American architect Nader Khalili (1936–2008) stand out. In the 1970s, Khalili abandoned his lucrative design business in Los Angeles and returned home for a five-year research odyssey amid Iran's vernacular settlements. Soon after, Khalili embarked on a new design project. Using clay, water, and fire, he invented the Geltaftan system, a renewed approach to conventional methods of kiln firing. After extensive trial and error, he sought to improve the structural weaknesses of existing adobe architectures by enhancing their resistance to earthquakes. Khalili's work in Iran resulted in a series of building projects (including the sandbag shelters of the 1990s and early 2000s) that were made cheaply and ecologically and were particularly apt for the immediate and temporary accommodation of refugees and disaster victims.

However, by the architect's own account, in the political atmosphere of the late-1970s and early 1980s, the world was more fascinated by the future than the present. So, Khalili translated his humanitarian "earth architecture" into shelters for lunar surfaces. In 1984 at a NASA-sponsored symposium on the future of lunar outposts, Khalili proposed a method for constructing lunar base structures in situ, by using unprocessed regolith. In this, he envisioned ceramic modules to be "thrown" on a centrifugally gyrating platform, allowing for direct interaction with the regolith while working to economical and technical advantage by using primarily local lunar resources. The result would be a regolith settlement in the form of a circular structure with radiating apses, resembling the floor plans of Persian adobe pigeon towers.

Khalili's sustainable proposal was in stark contrast with the proposals set forth at the same panel by contemporaneous construction experts. Noteworthy is a proposed project by a representative from the Portland Cement Company for setting up a cement factory on the moon to build office building types. Indeed, Khalili's humble, yet affective proposal was ahead of its time. While Khalili's ideas were published in his memoirs and a few scientific and architectural journals, they were never realized. Yet, as we pass the fiftieth anniversary of the Apollo 11 landing, Khalili's visions are more relevant than ever before. NASA, ESA, the Russian space agency, and Roscosmos are all pursuing the development of 3D printing technology to use the lunar regolith to 3D print lunar bases, echoing Khalili's lunar building methods from decades before. The futuristic lunar dream of Khalili for a sustained life is alive and well after all, it seems, as they were thirty some years ago.

Pamela Karimi is an Associate Professor of history of art and architecture at the University of Massachusetts Dartmouth and the author of *Domesticity and Consumer Culture in Iran* (Routledge, 2013). Her second monograph on contemporary alternative art scenes in Iran will be published in 2022 by Stanford University Press. A third book project on oil crisis, the Middle East, and the US quest for outer space settlements is in progress.

Nader Khalili's *Geltaftan* method in action in a village in Iran, 1982.

Nader Khalili's plan for habitation and workspace on lunar surfaces for seventy people, utilizing sun-and-shade zones and seven-circle compaction pattern to create maximum space with minimum material: (left) site plan; and (right) detail of crater base habitation. From Nader Khalili, "Lunar Structures Generated and Shielded with On-Site Materials," *The Journal of Aerospace Engineering* 2/3 (1984): 119–129.

A prototype for sandbag shelters under construction, Ahvaz, Iran, 1995.

FROM USSR'S NEFT DASHLARI TO SPACEX'S VOYAGER STATION: ARCHITECTURE IN RUIN

The ever-increasing colonization of nature by humans for the sake of productivity has turned vast territories into standardized technological landscape mutations. The modern scale of settlement transgresses the boundaries of the nation-state, taking on global dimensions. Today, companies such as Blue Origin are already speculating on establishing human settlements in space. SpaceX's Voyager Station is the latest architectural representation of such ambitions: the first hotel facility orbiting in space, it serves as an alternative vacation destination for the uber-rich. In this hyper-capitalist mode of architectural production, the balance or lack thereof seems to lie between economic and material forces at play. That is, how much capital extraction in one form (resources) and accumulation in another (commodity) can we accept under the pretext of a better future for humanity, while demorphing the earth and the world in general?

One explicit example of the intrinsic relationship between territories of resource extraction and the resulting built environment is Neft Dashlari or Oil Rocks, a monumental artificial island in the Caspian Sea. This self-proclaimed eighth wonder of the world was the first offshore oil drilling facility and industrial city. Built on water and land rich in oil and gas deposits in 1949, it was once the Stalinist utopia for the working class. Eight-story apartment blocks, along with a soccer pitch, library, three-hundred-seat cinema, and park made this steel and timber megastructure home to over five thousand workers in its heyday. Though the project is site-specific, its conception and ambition were also territorial if not global, tying the site to the Soviet territory and beyond. The Space Age years that followed the establishment of Neft Dashlari saw the emergence of cosmic architecture, as the Soviet state poured money into space exploration. The resulting projects not only expressed a rebirth of imagination that extended far beyond modernist conceptions of space, but also revealed a strong commitment to the formal role of architecture. Today, as resources around the island deplete, this still partially inhabited site is *in ruin*, gradually being submerged by the rising sea levels. And, while Neft Dashlari was once proudly represented on a Soviet stamp disseminated across the different republics, today, it has been removed from Google Maps.

With so much political power ceded to the tech industry in Silicon Valley, what is clear from initial architectural renderings is that without revisiting the goals and intentions of such projects, the spectacle celebrating SpaceX's Voyager Station and its successors will surely follow the fate of Neft Dashlari. As we engage in architectural production that is not even situated in a defined space, we must acknowledge the amount of power embodied in a space that is mediated and maintained through a technological platform. Today's ruling powers no longer maintain their power through the ownership of land. The power class of our time owns and controls data.

Given the increasing global popularization of quasi-fascist ideologies, and the continuous aestheticization of politics for popular gain, the complex relationship between architecture and politics and the culpability of architecture in representing totalitarian political regimes is as relevant today as it was in the last century. In this context, we are reminded of Walter Benjamin's still timely warning of the dangers allowing spectacle to infiltrate politics, and through it, architecture.[1] Today's ruins, such as Neft Dashlari, should be a means to decode a truth hidden beneath layers of romantic aestheticization of the object. They are a testimony to the interrelations between aesthetics, politics, and architecture, and their succumbing to the ravages of time. If the tower form manifests the universality of human knowledge with the specificity induced by the local, physical situation of the tower, how do we represent today the imposed globality of the world, and the false unity of its inhabitants?[2] What kind of platforms of representation do we rely on?

Garine Boghossian is an architect and urbanist based in New York. Her professional work experience includes large-scale urban and regional planning projects worldwide. Garine earned a post-professional degree in architecture and urbanism from the Massachusetts Institute of Technology. She has taught architecture and urban design studios at Northeastern University and the Boston Architectural College. She is currently an urbanist at ORG Permanent Modernity, New York office.

Soviet stamp showing Neft Dashlari, 1971.

Screenshot from Google Earth on the location of Neft Dashlari, 2021.

1   Walter Benjamin, *The Origin of German Tragic Drama*, trans. John Osborne (London: New Left Books, 1977).
2   Pierre Chabard, "Towers and Globes: Architectural and Epistemological Differences between Patrick Geddes's Outlook Towers and Paul Otlet's Mundaneums," in *European Modernism and the Information Society: Informing the Present, Understanding the Past*, ed. W. Boyd Rayward, 105–126 (London: Routledge, 2017).

GARINE BOGHOSSIAN

THE RUINS OF THE PRESENT

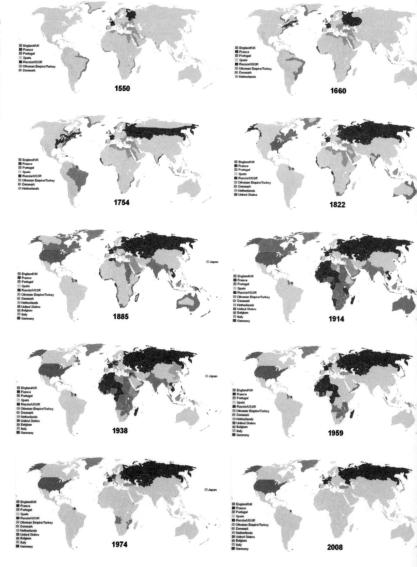

Histories, theories, and practices of architecture and urbanism are intimately interrelated to processes of colonialization. The world's territories and people have been constantly and continuously perturbed and marked by violent activities of war, occupation, exploitation, dispossession, destruction, and construction. Since the fifteenth century, Western European architects, both civil and military, have been actively participating in constructing empires and framing their representations. These designers were commissioned to imagine and realize various infrastructures, public buildings, and private settlements across the multiple territories of the empires they worked for. The vastness and diversity of colonial spaces around the world that resulted from these conditions have been instrumental in settling in the colonized land, exploiting and transporting resources, and representing an unevenly distributed power.

In his book, *Colonialism in Question: Theory, Knowledge, History,* US historian Frederick Cooper refuses to locate the colonial world between 1492 and the 1970s, arguing that "the globalization story claims as new what is not new at all, confuses 'long-distance' with 'global,' fails to complement discussion of connections across space with analysis of their limitations, and distorts the history of empires and colonization in order to fit it into a story with a predetermined end."[1] In spite of the fact that empires have a gigantic place and space in history and their changing maps cover a huge portion of the world, they are barely discussed and studied in Western European and North American architecture schools and departments. To this end, if the deeds of empires—the demarcation of borders; the design and construction of infrastructure, spaces, and systems of discipline, punishment, and exploitation; the imposition of boundaries and behaviors; the infliction of constructed narratives and representations; the toxification of environments; and the targeted destruction of built environments—are not taken seriously in architecture education, then architecture students and architects will tend to ignore these histories, maintain the ways in which powerful corporations and states act and operate today, and sustain the uneven exploitation and distribution of resources, capital, and labor.

Stories of globalization are an extension of histories of colonization. An effort to understand architecture, its histories and theories, as an integral part of the dynamics of the world's order and disorder rather than simply as a passive spectator and supplier of space, is fundamental. Such attention should neither evade the inherent violence of exploitation—human, animal, material, immaterial, territorial, atmospheric, underground, and environmental—nor fetishize it. Architecture operates on a planetary scale and depends on accumulated and distributed capital. The historical proximity of colonialization and globalization, and other forms of dispossession and violence, suggests that both colonization and globalization should speak to architects, architectural historians, and theorists. Unlike other disciplines and professions, architecture is a visible part of the landscape of the territories on which architectural projects have been designed and realized. It is a carrier of particular sociocultural and politico-economic histories and signifiers. Built environments are open-air archives. Both liberated and colonized lands contain the physical presence of these "ruins of the present," which need to be processed in order to better live together.

SAMIA HENNI

Samia Henni is an architectural historian and Assistant Professor at Cornell University. She is the author of the multi-award-winning *Architecture of Counterrevolution: The French Army in Northern Algeria* (gta Verlag, 2017), the editor of *War Zones* (gta papers 2), and the curator of *Housing Pharmacology/Right to Housing* and *Discreet Violence: Architecture and the French War in Algeria*.

Maps indicating the territories colonized by European powers, the United States, and Japan. Years shown: 1550, 1660, 1754, 1822, 1885, 1914, 1938, 1959, 1974, and 2008. June 23, 2008 (original upload date).

1   Frederick Cooper, *Colonialism in Question: Theory, Knowledge, History* (Berkeley, CA: University of California Press, 2005), 10.

PETER G. ROWE

SHARED EXPERIENCE AND APPRECIATION OF ARCHITECTURAL QUALITIES

As a *modus operandi*, "*how will we live together?*" can occur through shared experience and appreciation of architectural qualities. Furthermore, it would seem that the likelihood of such sharing would be enhanced significantly by the prominence and distribution of the qualities on offer and the ability for them to be comprehended and thus appreciated. This would also appear to be most possible from a cosmopolitan vantage point, where one's own inherent habits of mind remain intact while deeply appreciating those of others, in the manner of walking in the shoes of another without losing sight of one's own point of view.[1]

At its core cultural cosmopolitanism converges onto a singular outlook that rejects exclusive attributes of a particular, national culture, while appreciating and embracing a multicultural *mélange*. Nevertheless, as suggested above, a true cosmopolitan would also retain an affinity towards his or her own culture while deepening or broadening that affinity by knowing well the culture of others. In architecture the mode of cultural appreciation varies. In the West, for instance, it is rather strongly drawn toward finite objects and their attributes, while in Japan it accedes toward infinite processes, and in China toward an expansive, Confucian-based, Daoist, and Buddhist-tinged "art of living."[2]

In addition, the architectural qualities that come to mind should be universally approachable, even if relatively unknown, like the quality of light and the particularities of degrees in its shadowing. Moreover, recall and memory play a vital role, first to allow registry of specific qualities and then to conjure up prior experiences such that connections are drawn and necessary enlargements, distortions, and edits are made in order to render qualitative readings that are larger than life— at least at the moment of being observed and in the mind's eye of the observer.

The accompanying image, titled *Texas Remembered*, is part of a triptych by the late Lauretta Vinciarelli, an architect and noted artist. It is a fictional depiction not of architecture *per se*, but of evidence that it exists.[3] Taken together with a cosmopolitan outlook or a willingness to become absorbed in the architectural landscape, the sublime character of balance, reflection, irradiation, and natural and other circumstances

98

Peter G. Rowe is the Raymond Garbe Professor of Architecture and Urban Design at the Graduate School of Design, Harvard University where he is also a Harvard University Distinguished Service Professor. The author, co-author or editor of 25 books about architecture and urban design, he served as Dean of the Faculty of Design at Harvard from 1992 to 2004.

provides the basis for genuine and heartfelt exchange so necessary to living together. One can also imagine a dialog in which she says, "It could be like this," to which he responds, "Yes, but shouldn't it be like this," and the passersby readily agrees.

1   See Kwame Anthony Appiah, *Cosmopolitanism: Ethics in a World of Strangers* (New York: W. W. Norton, 2006).

2   See Augustin Berque, *Vivre l'espace au Japon* (Paris: Presses Universitaires de France, 1982) and Zehou Li, *The Chinese Aesthetic Tradition* (Honolulu, HI: University of Hawai'i Press, 2010).

3   See *Not Architecture but Evidence That It Exists: Lauretta Vinciarelli, Watercolors*, ed. Brooke Hodge (New York: Princeton Architectural Press, 1998). Image is in the private collection of Peter G. Rowe, NY, New York.

Laura Vinciarelli, *Texas Remembered* (series 3 of 3), 1988. Windsor and Newton watercolor on paper, 30 × 20 inches.

PETER G. ROWE

EUROPEAN-
NESS

Politically speaking, Europe today is seen as fragile and controversial entity. It is threatened by financial crisis, low-rate politicians, economic and ecologic crisis, and a growing gap between the rich and the poor. And now the pandemic. But Europe is also a *space*. A space of growing importance exactly for the same reasons that generate its decline and that makes it into a typical battlefield for contemporary spatial and political conflict. From being the nest for the artistic *avant-garde*, Europe has now evolved into the frontline of a different sphere of human phenomena: migration, climate change, cultural and political regression, industrial and welfare crises, and impossible dialog between individuals and groups from different social classes.

After the end of World War II, Europe's acknowledged values, which had survived twentieth-century tragedies, consisted of very precise *spatial* projections: cities, buildings, landscapes, streets, and piazzas—physical and institutional social spaces. In the postwar period, such spaces were instantly redefined as heritage and contributed to preserving the sense of coexistence and civilization Europeans wanted to consider at the core of their identity. The same urban and architectural heritage formed one of the pillars of the political utopia that is today's European Union (EU), which was built by farsighted politicians to prevent Europeans countries from falling back into its past horrors. *La città europea* therefore became not only a definition for a specific type of urban conglomeration but also the name for a global system of values aiming at preserving the role of public space, civic architecture, spatial welfare, and social facilities contributing to a modern and tolerant idea of democracy.

Monuments, institutional buildings, and people's spaces (basically *L'architettura della città*, according to Aldo Rossi) cooperated idealistically in shaping an open society where conflict was also a necessary agent of progress. What we're seeing today, at the core of Europe, is a rupture in this system of cooperation. Trading space for politics, we could say that a large percentage of citizens have started to see the institutional buildings representing EU mainly as the spatial metaphor of a privileged and self-protecting elite. In this fractured space between EU lovers and EU haters (the Brexit syndrome!), bad politics and harsh conflict take center stage, shadowing the cultural and political role Europe used to play and needs to play once again—a role grounded in tolerance, advanced democracy, accessible education, and health care, among other things.

It is interesting though that some signals of a renewed discussion about Europe as a space seem to rise from the horizon of "young architecture." It is a discussion that started about fifteen years ago, though was quickly interrupted by the financial and migration crisis, at a time when Rem Koolhaas was often paired with Romano Prodi in official photos and AMO was proudly publishing a *History of Europe and the European Union*. In 2018 the Belgian pavilion at the 16th International Architecture Exhibition of La Biennale di Venezia was turned by the Belgian-French team Traumnovelle into *Eurotopie*, an open arena for dialogue and political-architectural confrontation. Outside the gate of the same Biennale, an Italian team (Supervoid + Anna Livia Friel) loudly advocated for the need to build an *EU pavilion*—a space in which to investigate the role of architecture culture in rebuilding and redefining European identity. It could be said that in order to return to Europe its role as a "feasible utopia" we need to expand the list of buildings and spaces that make Europe a place where we will like to live together. Not only traditional civic and welfare architecture, but also decent spaces for refugees, facilities for integration, sensible design strategies for climate and the environment, heritage management, innovative workspaces and so forth. In this way Europe may be the essential ally we need in the delicate debate on democracy that will inevitably take place in the years to come.

Pippo Ciorra is an architect, critic, and Professor at SAAD (University of Camerino) and director of the PhD program "Villard d'Honnecourt." Author of books and essays, he was part of the curatorial team for the 1991 Venice Architecture Biennale and juror for the 2016 edition. He has curated exhibitions in Italy and abroad. Since 2009, he is the Senior Curator of MAXXI Architettura in Rome.

PIPPO CIORRA

Supervoid Architects and Anna Livia Friel, EUPavilion, EUPavilion Campaign based on Arduino Cantafora's depiction of G. Selva's gardens in Venice, 2019.

THE BARDO

The Arab Spring began in Tunisia. Public protests followed the self-immolation of Mohamed Bouazizi, a frustrated fruit seller, in December 2010, and led to the departure of the nation's dictator, Zine el-Abidine Ben Ali, less than a month later. The events that followed shook the world, mostly for the worse. In Egypt, a dictator was deposed and replaced by a democratically elected Islamist, himself deposed and replaced by a new dictator. In Yemen, Libya, and Syria, uprisings led to civil war that has not yet ended. The last of these sparked a refugee crisis arguably unparalleled since the 1940s, one which, in turn contributed to the breakdown of the European Union's Schengen Agreement on open borders and to the rise of xenophobic populism in Europe and the United States.

Yet in Tunisia, where it all began, something completely different happened. An elected constituent assembly convened in the Bardo, a nineteenth-century, neo-Moorish, Beylical palace expanded in the twentieth century to feature two large national legislative chambers. Working for almost three years—negotiating, arguing, and compromising in the shadow of the disasters unfolding elsewhere—the assembly managed to agree on a democratic constitution, one that enshrines freedom and equality for all Tunisians and protects both religious liberty and the separation of religion from the state. The Tunisian people ratified it in 2014.

The work was extremely difficult, and the compromise repeatedly came close to failing. Two politicians were assassinated during the process, one of them an assembly member. Nor was the Bardo itself spared. In 2015, terrorists associated with the Islamic State attacked the National Museum housed in the same complex, killing twenty-one people and wounding some fifty more.

Nevertheless, the Tunisian constitution, produced in the drafting rooms of the Bardo, discussed in its members's cafeteria, and formally adopted in its assembly hall, stands as a testament to what thoughtful, reasonable, patient people can accomplish when they aim to live together. Today Tunisia is a functioning constitutional democracy, the first in the Arabic-speaking world. It has now transferred power multiple times via peaceful elections. Democratic Tunisia is not perfect, and it is only a decade old by the longest possible reckoning. It does, however, exist; that is itself no small accomplishment.

The name "Bardo," said to be derived from the Spanish "prado" (an open, grassy expanse), captures Tunisia's cosmopolitan, Mediterranean legacy. The complex is rambling and multiuse. For a long time, at least until the terrorist attack, it was easily accessible (perhaps, in retrospect, too easily): if the gate leading to the assembly building was locked, you could drive or walk around the perimeter to the museum entrance; come in there; and walk a few feet to the assembly through the rear staircase.

The framers of constitutions like to think of themselves as architects, building so that we may live together. The blueprints are made of compromise and consensus. The structures are designed to evolve and adapt with time. When well made, the edifices are hardly noticed. When, ill-made, they crumble and fall, the effects are felt everywhere.

Noah Feldman is a Professor of Law and Chairman of the Society of Fellows at Harvard University. He's a member of the Academy of Arts and Sciences, contributing writer for *Bloomberg View*, and the host of the podcast, "Deep Background with Noah Feldman." He's also the author of nine books including his forthcoming, *The Broken Constitution: Lincoln, Slavery, and the Refounding of America* (Farrar, Straus and Giroux).

EP President Martin Schulz delivers a speech at the Assembly of the Representatives of the People, Tunisia, 2016.

ARCHITECTURE
IN THE AGE OF
MIGRATIONS

We live in the century of migrations. However, current laws and values that organize international relations fall short of imagining a just, cosmopolitan world. Rather than rethinking the border systems that block equality in migrations, world authorities are reacting with anti-immigrant and nationalist policies that perpetuate the *status quo*. As I am editing this text in the midst of the coronavirus pandemic in the US, migrants who are deemed illegal are doing the essential jobs for the society that make them more vulnerable, and it is common to hear opportunistic predictions for the future that endorse isolation and xenophobia, rather than learn the lessons to institute global health equality. Architects who are committed to justice and diversity, instead, can respond with open architecture—the translation of a new ethics of hospitality toward the immigrant into the process of design, the welcoming of another mind into one's own.[1]

While architects have not paid enough attention to the ethics and politics of international migration, which would involve expanding human rights and social citizenship through space, there are nonetheless some latent modes of open architecture in history that one could build upon. These examples demonstrate that there are indeed formal, procedural, and programmatic ways of designing open architecture by considering, for instance, the flexibility and adaptability of form, collaboration and collectivity during the design process, participation and radical democracy in decision making, anticipation of the multiplicity of meaning, open-sourceable design, and so on. Actually, architecture is by definition open, in the sense that buildings are always appropriated by their habitants whether their architects have anticipated or forbidden these changes. Yet, it is not appropriability and interpretability that distinguish an open-work from a closed one, but rather the intentionally unfinished nature of the built-form that awaits habitant completion. While buildings and spaces always get activated with the life that emerges in them, open architecture takes place when architects embrace new qualities of openness during the stage of design.

For example, the urban renewal and habitation of the immigrant neighborhood Kreuzberg in Berlin since the 1980s is a case in point, which raises questions about the emergence and contradictions of some latent open architectures in history, and helps us understand immigrant agency in shaping world cities. For this urban renewal initiative, Hardt-Waltherr Hämer and his team including Heide Moldenhauer and Cihan Arın sought ways of translating radical democracy into architecture by employing participatory renewal without displacing current immigrant residents; Álvaro Siza prescribed zones for residents' voices at the design stage; Aldo Rossi, Josef Paul Kleihues, and Rob Krier improved their ideas on collective memory and will, as well as collaborative urban design; Frei Otto offered a tree-like set of platforms on which residents built their idiosyncratic houses; John Hejduk conceptualized architecture as an evolving, performative stage with unfamiliar spaces; Herman Hertzberger undertook a self-help project where units were finalized by cooperative members; and Rem Koolhaas and AMO imagined Berlin as a visual history of its own non-actualized possibility. Many of these practices, however, fell short in responding to the immigrant character of Kreuzberg, threatened by the Berlin Senate's contemporary discriminatory housing laws and regulations for demographic engineering, such as moving bans and immigrant quotas. That is why Kreuzberg is also an excellent example of immigrant agency against all odds. In the case of the lack of hospitality reflected in architecture, many immigrant habitants triumphed over non-open spaces by making them their own, such as carving up kitchens and bedrooms out of surplus spaces designed for the sake of signature form. Today, in the context of the threat of gentrification, many immigrants rightfully take credit of Kreuzberg's urban renewal and its symbolic significance in the global imagination by pointing out their own financial and cultural contributions in making the area one of the most cosmo-politan, creative, and politically engaged places to live in the world.

Esra Akcan is the author of *Landfill Istanbul: Twelve Scenarios for a Global City*; *Architecture in Translation: Germany, Turkey and the Modern House* (124/3, 2004); *Turkey: Modern Architectures in History* (with S. Bozdoğan, Reaktion Books, 2012); and *Open Architecture: Migration, Citizenship and the Urban Renewal of Berlin-Kreuzberg by IBA-1984/87* (Birkhäuser, 2018). Her works offer new ways to understand the global movements and migrations of architecture, and advocate a commitment to social, global, and environmental justice.

View of the void space in Karaçizmeli's apartment appropriated as a kitchen, in Álvaro Siza's *Bonjour Tristesse* building for IBA-1984/87, Berlin, 2012.

View of an apartment in Block 81 in Kreuzberg showing an additional room appropriated from the neighboring building and stairs negotiating the level difference, Berlin, 2020.

1   For a discussion on open architecture, see Esra Akcan, *Open Architecture: Migration, Citizenship and the Urban Renewal of Berlin-Kreuzberg by IBA-1984/87* (Basel, Switzerland: Birkhäuser-deGruyter, 2018).

THE LAYERED CITY

Though it starred Jude Law and Juliette Binoche, *Breaking and Entering* is one of Antony Minghella's lesser known films. It conveys something important and perhaps uncomfortable about the nature of city life. Jude Law plays a successful landscape architect with a studio in a sandblasted brick warehouse in the midst of London's King's Cross. It's a district in transition, which by night is overtaken by Albanian drug dealers who break in to steal his computers, and Nigerian cleaners who he pays to clean up the mess that they leave behind.

Through this film, King's Cross is seen as a reflection of the city as a multilayered environment in which very different groups of people exist side by side in the same space but hardly acknowledge each other's existence. It demonstrates the brutal speed with which the contemporary city is changing, and perhaps also the way in which the pace of that change freezes out the diversity that is the mark of a living city.

There are other parts of London that suggest a different kind of urban life and potential. Brick Lane is a front line between an expanding financial district spreading eastward, and one of the city's poorest districts, yet it maintains qualities and capacities that King's Cross has lost. It is still a place that can accommodate migrants with no resources beyond the determination to make a new life for themselves, find a home and work; as they prosper, they have the chance to move on.

What is now a mosque at 59 Brick Lane, on the corner of Fournier Street, was once a synagogue and before that a Methodist chapel, but it was originally built as Huguenot place of worship in 1743. If one single building can represent the essence of London's cultural diversity over three centuries, this is it. Brick Lane, now the center of the city's Bangladeshi community, was once an area of weavers' lofts—domestic family factories run by protestant refugees from France's murderous religious wars. Their presence lingers only in a few additions to the area's eighteenth-century houses, built for their looms by the Huguenots, and in the form of the brick building on the corner of Brick Lane and Fournier street.

This building has a stainless-steel minaret and today, it is an Islamic place of worship. It was built by the French in plain but handsome classical brick style. In between its life as a chapel and a mosque it was, for more than a century, a synagogue—established by eastern European Jews fleeing Russian pogroms.

The transformation of this one building is mirrored by that of the city around it.

A few doors down, the pavements are still crowded with touts handing out flyers for curry houses, and shops selling saris outside a 1960s office slab that has been transformed into the kind of workplace designed with a start-up economy in mind given its carefully selected collections of mismatched mid-century modern furniture, and its curated evening events. Brick Lane's street signs, now rendered in Bengali as well as in English, can be seen either as a mark of respect to the Bangladeshi migrants who came to London in the 1970s, or as a piece of marketing-led branding as condescending as the pagoda roofs on the phone booths in San Francisco's Chinatown. But this is still a fluid city, a part of London which remains open to possibilities.

Deyan Sudjic is Director Emeritus of the Design Museum, London, and Professor of Architecture and Design Studies at Lancaster University. He is a curator, editor, and critic, director of the Venice Architecture Biennale in 2002, editor of *Domus* (2000–2003), and founding editor of *Blueprint* magazine. His most recent book, *The Language of Cities*, was published by Penguin in 2017.

DEYAN SUDJIC

Brick Lane Jamme Masjid in Tower Hamlets, London, 2019.

111

LIVING TOGETHER: CHICKENS ON OPIUM AND ICE

In the summer of 1898, residents of my ancestral home, a small village called Deh 22 in central Sindh, then part of British India, found themselves unwittingly sharing the contents of their meals with another village across the world, Little Compton in Rhode Island, which incidentally is my current home. Something curious transpired between the two places, an unlikely link that kept intact a supply of the most unusual ingredients across the ocean: chickens and ice.

This improbable passage was inscribed on water with blood. Providence, before it started shipping ice and chickens to India, was the epicenter of the North American slave trade. What gave enterprises like the Browns's and the DeWolfs's a winning edge was their fast ships, including record-holding schooners that completed the Middle Passage. Eventually, however, speed couldn't outrun violence. The rising abolitionist movements made the trade morally, if not economically, untenable.

Brown's schooners, however, were not to lay dormant. The late eighteenth century marked the beginning of a global tea fever. While the Chinese authorities refused to trade in anything but silver, the British East India Company hatched a notorious scheme, which would turn the tide. It couldn't grow tea in India, but it could grow opium. An elaborate agricultural and industrial setup was put in place in Bengal to grow, process, and smuggle opium to China by sea to obtain Chinese silver from an ever-increasing addicted population. The Company expanded production, allowing independent British merchants to set up trade houses turning fortunes in Bengal and Canton. The opium trade not only made tea available in Britain, it started draining China itself of silver.

Initially, the Providence merchants could only dip their toes in the opium trade, until the Chinese market exploded in the 1820s, increasing demand to such an extent that the British couldn't hold monopoly on exports. Seeing a window of opportunity, the Browns' fast schooners started crossing the ocean in record times to smuggle opium from India into China.

What should be taken to India on the long voyage across the Atlantic? One unusual scheme was put forth by a Boston businessman, Frederick Tudor, famously known as the "Ice King." Tudor was set on calculating if his ice would survive the trip across the Atlantic. to reach a much bigger market of overheated Company men and native elite in India. Harvested from frozen ponds in thin layers and stacked atop each other like pancakes, the Ice King's ice filled the narrowly separated berths in the hulls of the very ships that had carried prone and shackled bodies of slaves only a short while ago. The ice not only

113

survived the improbable months-long passage through ocean heat and humidity, but also lasted through the Indian summer stored in newly constructed massive ice houses at ports like Chennai. Much of it ended up in ceilings of specially outfitted colonial bungalows.

Sometime in the late 1870s, one Isaac Champlin Wilbour of Little Compton claimed, to have raised a new breed of chicken that not only produced meat quickly, but would continue to give large quantities of eggs if not eaten. This fortunate production was also tied to links half way across the world. A host of "oriental" chickens, from Cochin, Java, Malay, and Shanghai had been hitching rides aboard ships inbound from opium runs for over half a century, yielding several robust variants, one of which Wilbour crossed with the Italian Brown Leghorn to result in the Rhodie. By the 1890s, Rhodies from Rhode Island and ice from Walden Pond had found their way even to small villages like Deh 22.

These villages with curious numbers for names were part of another unlikely scheme. The rising tension leading up to the American Civil War diminished the supply of US cotton to Britain, causing the famous "Lancashire cotton famine" of 1867. The wealth accumulated through the long opium trade, however, made it plausible to dig hundreds of miles of irrigation canals in the desert in Sindh and transplant small farmers from the northern Punjab to start another cotton supply chain. This forced movement of soil, silt, and seeds would too spill blood when met by a rebelling indigenous Hur population.

Rhodie, Rhodie, Rhodie, I remember my great grandmother calling the chickens at feeding time. The name of the vermilion red birds that gathered around her feet was native to her Punjabi. And who was to say it wasn't? When ice and chickens, opium and tea, water and cotton had travelled across the ocean for a century to quench the quivering lips of addicts and connoisseurs, slave owners and imperialists, hungry farmers and sailors alike, the lines between living together and living apart had forever been blurred.

Ijlal Muzaffar is an Associate Professor of Architectural History and the Director of the graduate program in Global Arts and Cultures at the Rhode Island School of Design. His work explores how the global has been imagined through various colonial and postcolonial geographies, from the slave, opium, cotton, and ice trades to Third World development.

The Rhode Island Red, the chicken that crossed the ocean. Image from Dwight Edward Hale, *Standard-Bred Rhode Island Reds, Rose and Single Comb, Their Practical Qualities, The Standard Requirements, How to Judge Them, How to Mate and Breed for Best Results* (Buffalo, NY: American Poultry Publishing Company, 1911).

Frederic Tudor's ice harvesting operation near Cambridge, Massachusetts, which, at its height in 1833, shipped ice to India.

THE
ADVENTIVE
SPECIES

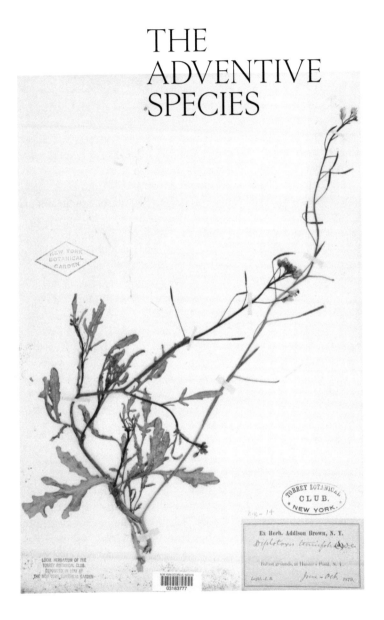

NEW YORK
BOTANICAL
GARDEN

LOCAL HERBARIUM OF THE
TORREY BOTANICAL CLUB.
DEPOSITED IN 1896 AT
THE NEW YORK BOTANICAL GARDEN

TORREY BOTANICAL
CLUB.
NEW YORK.

Ex Herb. Addison Brown, N. Y.

Ballast grounds, at Hunter's Point, N. Y.

03183777

During the late nineteenth century, gentlemen botanists Aubrey Smith of Philadelphia and Addison Brown of New York organized plant collecting expeditions and surveys at the waterfront edges of their expanding metropolises. They were fascinated by the unexpected botanical specimens emerging from these so-called waste lands or "ballast grounds," which sprouted from seeds inadvertently transported with the ballast materials of gravel, soil, and rubble and shipped in the holds of transatlantic clipper ships making their way to North America. In an early enactment of real estate speculation, these materials were dumped to create new land at the cities' marginal water lots, and the latent seeds took hold. Pressed into herbarium specimen books and surveyed for consecutive years, the botanists championed these novel plants as "waifs from abroad" and bemoaned their loss to subsequent urban "improvements."[1] Yet in a report to the Torrey Botanical Club, Addison Brown remained optimistic: "While most of them will therefore perish after a few seasons, sufficient opportunity will nevertheless be afforded to some, not hitherto reported here, to test their endurance of our climate and to compete with our native growths. The less hardy plants will be ejected by our vigorous weeds; but *Atriplex rosea*, *A. laciniata*, and *Diplotaxis tenuifolia*, and doubtless others, will maintain their ground."[2]

Dubbed "adventive flora" by the American botanists, these fragile colonies of plant pioneers hailed from Europe, Africa, Asia, South America, and the West Indies, and emerged throughout the wastelands and ballast grounds of the Atlantic seaboard.[3] The term "adventive" describes a species that has arrived in a new locality from a different habitat, usually introduced with the help—intentional or otherwise—of humans. *Adventive* poetically conjures up the word *inventive* and is certainly a more positive moniker than "alien," "invasive," or "foreign" as a term describing these opportunistic species that quickly adapted to nineteenth-century ruderal environments and disturbed grounds. But by the early 1900s, federal legislation defining "noxious weeds" and controlling the entry of plants into the United States was enacted. Interestingly, immigration reform acts also surged at this time, ostensibly to prevent disease transmission but also "racial taint." Uncannily similar language was employed for both plants and humans. Yet evolution, like immigration, never rests, and even weeds are capable of adaptive speciation, evolving into new and distinct species. We have much to learn from these "plants as inventors."[4] The adaptability of ballast plants provides them with the very characteristics necessary to thrive in a future climate scenario.

As Ralph Waldo Emerson asserted, a weed is "a plant whose virtues have not yet been discovered."[5] The longstanding, foiled attempt by humans to control and attack weeds has produced in these plants genetic strategies of diversity and resilience, as opposed to the controlled yet vulnerable populations of deliberately bred genetic clones produced by agricultural crop and horticultural nursery propagation. Weeds are opportunists, as observed by the ballast plant champions Aubrey Smith and Addison Brown, and are best described in their terms as adventive species, rather than aliens or exotics. Despite all odds, weeds manage to flourish in whatever habitat—disturbed or otherwise—is made available. Indeed, the paleontologist David Jablonsky argues that humans are the ultimate weedy species: aggressive, prolific, and ready to travel.[6] The plasticity and resilience of adventive flora—indeed, a queer ecology—presents an exemplary model of new, non-normative assemblages for living in a climate-adaptive future.

Catherine Seavitt Nordenson is a professor and director of the Graduate Landscape Architecture Program at the Spitzer School of Architecture, City College of New York. Her research examines the impacts of power, activism, and public health on equitable landscape design and policy. Recent publications include *Depositions: Roberto Burle Marx and Public Landscapes under Dictatorship* (University of Texas Press, 2018) and *Structures of Coastal Resilience* (Island Press, 2018).

Addison Brown, *Diplotaxis tenuifolia*, herbarium specimen collected at Hunter's Point, New York, 1879. Commonly known as perennial wall-rocket, wild rocket, Lincoln weed, or wild Italian arugula, this is a flowering plant of the mustard family Brassicaceae. Described by Brown as an "almost invariable index of ballast ground," this spontaneous plant was once considered a problematic "weed." It is now increasingly sought after as an edible salad herb, and its leaves have notable antioxidant and nutritional properties.

1   Addison Brown, "Ballast Plants in New York City and its Vicinity," in *Bulletin of the Torrey Botanical Club* 6, no. 59 (1879): 354.
2   Ibid.
3   Aubrey H. Smith, "On Colonies of Plants Observed near Philadelphia," in *Proceedings of the Academy of Natural Sciences of Philadelphia* 19 (1867): 15–24.
4   I borrow this exceptional phrase from the title of Raoul Heinrich France's *Die Pflanze als Erfinder* (Stuttgart: Kosmos, Gesellschaft der Naturfreunde, 1920). France's influential theory of the "biotechnic" sought to integrate biological processes with technology.
5   Ralph Waldo Emerson, "The Fortune of the Republic," in *The Complete Works of Ralph Emerson Waldo*, vol. 11, *Miscellanies* (Boston, MA: Houghton Mifflin, 1904), 512.
6   See David Quammen, "Planet of Weeds: Tallying the Losses of Earth's Animals and Plants," *Harper's Magazine*, October 1998, 57–69.

CATHERINE SEAVITT NORDENSON

117

BEYOND
BORDERS

The oyster beds in the north of Bahrain were the center of a natural pearl fishery that dominated the Persian Gulf from the third century BC until the early twentieth century. Despite the fact that pearl fishing was the main source of wealth for the economy of Bahrain until the 1930s, the oyster beds for which it was known were a shared resource amongst the neighboring countries, according to an ancestral tribal system that had been commonly practiced by these coastal populations for centuries.[1] At the start of each pearling season, dhow boats from countries across the Gulf would sail to the waters surrounding Bahrain to test their luck, moving from oyster bed to oyster bed during the annual three-month pearling season.

On land, the Bedouin tribes of the Arabian desert created a system of shared property, which concerned water distribution and the movement of herds and people across transnational borders, within a larger political system that accommodated the nomadic nature of the tribes.

In the mid-twentieth century, the notion of the nation-state was adopted and partially adapted to the countries of the Persian Gulf, confining nomadic migrations to fixed borders and boundaries. These ancient traditions uncomfortably adapted to this new sedimentary reality, either by confining their movements within the boundaries of the state they found themselves in or settling within urban settings. The exercise of the establishment of the nation-state was driven by the accrued wealth and increase of settlements bought by the pearling economy and later supported by the oil industry, which became the driving force of the various Gulf economies. Industries affiliated with the oil economy developed neatly within the confines of national borders; the resulting gas emissions did not. They followed a more nomadic route across land, sea, and crust and put a stress on local resources, mainly on the supply of fresh water and clean air. In turn, the shortage of affordable fresh water and arable land compelled many of these countries to report the problem of their food security beyond the confines of their local borders.[2]

This partial history of resources and emissions—while specific to the Persian Gulf—is symptomatic of wider issues and challenges facing the world. The inadequacy of current political models in the face of climate change seems obvious, and yet the alternatives are not. The negative impacts of our current lifestyle and economic models are trespassing national boundaries, calling for a shared and global response to climate change. At the same time, the increasing mobility of people—as travelers, tourists, migrants, wanderers, expatriates, and refugees— has reintroduced nomadism as an emergent global behavior. If humans, air particles, microplastics and viruses are increasingly defying the notion of national boundaries, then surely it is time to think of a new political order; one where ancestral nomadic traditions could serve as a starting point to imagine a system of governance that relies on a global understanding of resources and a novel approach to the relationship between citizenship and territory.

Noura Al Sayeh-Holtrop is an architect and curator currently working at the Bahrain Authority for Culture and Antiquities (BACA) as Head of Architectural Affairs. Noura was the co-curator of *Reclaim*, Bahrain's first participation at the 12th International Architecture Exhibition of La Biennale di Venezia in 2010 that was awarded a Golden Lion, and the Deputy Commissioner General for *Archaeologies of Green*. Since 2015, she heads the *Pearling, Testimony of an Island Economy* UNESCO World Heritage project, which has been awarded the Aga Khan Award for Architecture for the 2019 cycle.

NOURA AL SAYEH-HOLTROP

Dhow boats in the northern waters of Bahrain.

A pearling crew composed of the captain, haulers, and divers in the northern waters of Bahrain.

1   Robert A. Carter, *Sea of Pearls: Seven Thousand Years of the Industry That Shaped the Gulf* (London: Arabian, 2012).

2   In 2015, Bahrain purchased 42,000 hectares of land for agricultural purposes in Sudan, roughly half the size of its sovereign land. See "Bahrain to Invest in Sudan Agri Market," *Trade Arabia*, June 10, 2013, http://www.tradearabia.com /news/MISC_237546.html/.

PATCHY LANDSCAPES OF COEXISTENCE

The concept of patchiness is borrowed from landscape ecology, where a patch is defined as a structural unit of a broader environment, maintaining strong boundaries with its neighbors like a stance of trees growing in a prairie or a road driven through a dense forest.[1] While each patch is related to adjacent patches, the contact of their different ecological systems may be extremely low. A patchy landscape is an uneven distribution of activities in an environment increasingly fragmented and dominated by industrial activities. Such fragmentation challenges various modes of coexistence, both human and non-human, within and across patches. Focus on patchy landscapes draws attention to the unstable heterogeneity and entangled reactions of the earth's environment of land, air, water, and fire.

Climate change is altering patterns of persistence and coexistence across these patchy landscapes. The earth's environmental framework is in danger, and so too is that of cities and metropolitan regions. Dams, diversions, and toxic effluents erode river deltas and threaten modes of existence such as life along the lower Mississippi River and in New Orleans. Hazardous air pollution from burning coal, chemicals, and wooden materials blankets New Delhi with smog, creating irreversible lung damage in millions of children. The tornado-like wildfires of Australia have caused dozens of humans and billions of animals to perish. The fires have wrapped in smog the cities of Adelaide, Canberra, Melbourne, and Sydney. The list of local environmental damage creating global destruction goes on.

Yet the effects of these dangers are unevenly distributed across the globe, regions, and cities producing patchy landscapes. High polluting land-uses and toxic landfills are disproportionately located in low-income neighborhoods. Green spaces and water-front parks are seldom designed for those areas with the highest environmental risks. Communally-farmed land within cities tends to be ignored as productive of skills and income and viewed instead as residual patches of land withdrawn from development. Ineffective zoning ordinances allow residential development in wetlands and areas prone to flooding. Yet all of these long-neglected patches of land-use need careful attention lest remediation and restoration erase necessary differences and needs.

While acknowledging catastrophe, how do we understand the drivers of coexistence that form and reform these patchy landscapes? How do we learn to live beside and within these patches of difference? Can we learn to make room for others? Can we moderate the pro-growth development machine and our belief in techno-industrial innovations called progress, aimed to eradicate any patch of difference as residual, parasitic, or a holdback from necessary modernization?

How instead do we attend to coexistence and relational entanglements that enrich all of our existence? How do we visualize and represent different patches as they come into being, as they compete for dominance, as they resist and survive or are eliminated and destroyed? Dynamic entanglements cannot be seen from an orthogonal perspective, layering on a base map isolated cross-sections of environmental substances necessary for survival. We need an up-close on-the-ground perspective, totally new representational techniques, and different metaphors that affect our perception of and belief in patchy coexistence. We can no longer hide behind barrier walls, Big Data modeling, simplified universalizing theories of global sustainability—all of which avoid looking at differences, analyzing unjust exclusions, and considering the unruliness and uneven heterogeneity of landscape structures and their related patches.

M. Christine Boyer is the William R. Kenan Jr. Professor at the School of Architecture, Princeton University. M. Christine Boyer received her PhD and Masters in City Planning from Massachusetts Institute of Technology. She also holds a Master's of Science in Computer and Information Science from the University of Pennsylvania, The Moore School of Electrical Engineering. She continues in her research and teaching to combine these two interests: urbanism and computational theory.

Paying attention to the ordinary shape and force of a tree trunk as it encounters the hardened and static concrete in a New York City side-walk develops awareness of shifting human-non-human entanglements and their undecidable struggles for coexistence. It demands us to think beyond the either/or dichotomy that aims to dismember the forceful dynamics of the non-human and to pose in its place a question of how can we learn to live together, 2019.

1   This article is inspired by "Patchy Anthropocene: Frenzies and Afterlives of Violent Simplifications." Supplement, *Current Anthropology* 60, no. S20 (August 2019).

LIVING WITH
NON-HUMAN
ANIMALS

MIRÓ ZABRINI

In 2018, approximately 124 million tonnes of poultry were produced worldwide. The scaling-up of poultry production is not a result of traditional farming methods, but of farming's absorption into the industrial process in the postwar era.[1] Critical to this shift was a realization that an animal's health and welfare worked counter to growing profit: Animals went from being understood as subjects to consumable objects.

The Vencomatic Group, a leading Dutch agribusiness founded in 1983, offers innovative solutions for nest and aviary systems for poultry farms where chickens, turkeys, layers, ducks, and broilers are bred, raised, and housed in an efficient manner. The company's aviary systems can be up to six tiers high, allowing for a greater density of chickens in each building, while still staying within the limits established by the European Commission of twenty-one birds per square-metre. A single building can hold as many as 160,000 chickens, with some farm complexes in the Netherlands housing up to one million. A chicken is considered ready for slaughter within 32 to 36 days, when it has reached an ideal weight of 2 to 2.5 kg.[2] This cycle is repeated seven to eight times per year, with the average lifespan of a chicken reduced from eight years to seven weeks.

The Netherlands has the most advanced poultry production system, which includes new techniques in genetic selection, feeding, incubation, and slaughtering. Often these systems look at ways to minimize animal suffering and waste that occurs in industrial processes. Some factory farms, for instance, integrate all necessary facilities in one farming complex. Typically, the facilities for different processes are in separate and distant locations; transporting livestock is often stressful for animals, with many dying during transit. Other factory farms have reduced waste by using feed composed from leftover resources from the human food industry, curbing waste and reducing carbon emissions. Nevertheless, while conditions are more humane, they are exceptions rather than the norm in industrial farming practices.

In factory farming, architecture is deployed as a set of inflexible constraints, defined by market interest for a higher yield of animal protein at a lower cost, which in turn subjects the animal's body to hostile interventions and design processes: debeaking, growth hormones, antibiotics, manipulation of the circadian cycle through controlled and manipulated interior light, and limited access to outdoor pastures. Thus, the non-human animal body is forcibly altered to fit and survive in an architecture designed for maximal profits.

A Vencomatic brochure claims that their products are based upon a "thorough understanding of the needs of the birds" and "of the manager alike."[3] Yet factory farms conceptualize non-human animals as a simple protein for human consumption. Our lingering guilt towards how we treat other animals cannot be assuaged by our relationship to companion animals or pets, which are produced by selective breeding to have a set of desirable traits catered specifically to humans.

Reflecting on the environmental crisis we are facing today—animal farming being a leading global contributor to carbon emissions—it cannot be addressed only through optimizing resources or transforming economic processes but requires a reevaluation of the relationship we establish with others, non-human animals included.

Mirko Zardini is an architect, author, and curator. From 2005 to 2019 he was the Director of the Canadian Centre for Architecture (CCA) in Montreal. Among his publications are *Asfalto: Il carattere della cittá* (2003), *Sense of the City: An Alternative Approach to Urbanism* (2005), *Sorry, Out of Gas: Architectural Responses to the 1973 Oil Crisis* (2007), *Actions: What You Can Do with the City* (2008), *Imperfect Health: The Medicalization of Architecture* (2011), *It's All Happening So Fast* (2016), and *The Museum Is Not Enough* (2019).

Andy Byers, *Pig*, 2011. Sculpture 1:1. Paper, foam, and plastic.

Andy Byers, *Chicken*, 2011. Sculpture 1:1. Paper, foam, and plastic.

Andy Byers, *Cow*, 2011. Sculpture 1:1. Paper, foam, and plastic.

1   Dawne McCane, *Critical Animal Studies: An Introduction* (Albany, NY: New York Press, 2013), 9.

2   Mathilde Gérard, "Aux Pays-Bas, le poulet élevé sur étagères à la conquête du monde," *Le Monde*, August 31, 2019, https://www.lemonde.fr /planete/article/2019/08/31/aux-pays-bas-le -poulet-eleve-sur-etageres-a-la-conquete -du-monde_5504812_3244.html.

3   "Think Ahead with Poultry People," Vencomatic Group, Brochure, 2018, https:// www.vencomaticgroup.com/public/pdfs/2018 _Brochure_-_Layers_EN33.pdf.

COOKING
NEW WORLDS
IN AN URBAN
SYMBIOME

SAROSH A. KESARIA

Modern architecture and industrial agriculture were both sold to the public as technological miracles. Today, their feigned efficiencies come at a steep cost to the global climate, biodiversity, rural communities, and future generations. Industrial agriculture uses 75% of farmland to produce 30% of the world's food. Most of the world is fed by small farms that use only 25% of available land. 70% of all birds and 60% of all mammalian life on the planet are now factory produced for food.[1] This intensive production of food is premised on an entire typology of machinic architectures that have gone planetary—Concentrated Animal Feeding Operations (CAFOs), refrigeration and cold storage facilities, supertrawlers, agricultural robots, transportation hubs, and ports for the efficient transport of food across the globe. Demand for food in one part of the world stimulates the creation of fields of monoculture thousands of miles away. The ecological footprint of food, like that of buildings, remains unconscionable.

Can we simultaneously liberate food and buildings from extractive economies, from cheap labor embedded in the exploitation of workers of the Global South, and from all acts of ecological degradation? There is a growing interest in the larger context of food—its cultures and ethics. This is evident from the rise of the slow food movements, local food co-ops, biodynamic farming, permaculture, freeganism, and low carbon diets. What are the architectural manifestations of these new food movements that combine decolonization and ecological remediation?

The Urban Symbiome is one such localized experiment of degrowth and circular thinking. Located in the urban-periurban context of London, it can also serve as a template for 'Cooking New Worlds' across various geographies. It promotes acts of symbiosis and kinship toward a steady state economy. Instead of extractive construction, the Urban Symbiome reuses building materials through acts of urban mining. The modernism of steel and concrete is further replaced by mycelium, hemp, timber, and compressed earth. These allow for architectures of growth and decay.

The Urban Symbiome connects places for growing, preparing, and selling food through a novel alliance of citizen farmers, builders, scientists, ecologists, consumers, immigrants, birds, bees, bats, butterflies, fish, bacteria, viruses, and plants. It is at once a hybrid building and a networked landscape—a synthetic construct of the human and natural world. Unused and volunteered parcels of land—urban, peri-urban, and suburban spaces; building terraces and facades; defunct parking lots, lawns, golf courses, and sites of the old industrial age—are fused, de-paved, and activated across territories through myriad acts of commoning.

The Urban Symbiome is a biome: an eco-restorative network of pollinator corridors, foraging landscapes, and bioswales. It is a trove of biodiversity that generates its own microclimates. Anaerobic digestors convert food scraps and feces into energy for buildings and compost for plants. This forms a literal and ontological link between the scales of microbiota and those of geographical biomes. Far from a nostalgia for nature, the Urban Symbiome is tactical in its appropriation of the city. Decommissioned tunnels and air-raid bunkers perpetuate a landscape of vertical farms using aqua-, aero-, hydroponics where food is grown in the surreal, pink LED light.

The Urban Symbiome is an archetypal antidote to the global twentieth-century networks of planetary agriculture. It is an antithesis to sanitized *tabula rasa* modernism and its machinic efficiencies; it remains inefficient, partly feral, and of the ground.

Sarosh Anklesaria is a practicing architect, educator, and the T. David Fitz-Gibbon Professor of Architecture at Carnegie Mellon University. His work locates architectural agency across a range of scales, temporalities, and geographies. Recent projects have been supported by The Richard Rogers Fellowship, The Art Omi Residency, and the Taliesin Fellowship.

1   Yinon Bar-On, Rob Phillips, and Ron Milo, "The Biomass Distribution on Earth," *Proceedings of the National Academy of Sciences of the United Sates of America* 115, no. 25 (June 2018): 6506–6511.

Sarosh Anklesaria and Priyanka Sheth, *Cooking New Worlds in an Urban Symbiome*, 2020.

SPATIAL PEDAGOGY: CREATING THE COMMONS

What does it mean to inhabit the commons within a spatial and pedagogical practice?

She first visited Sweet Water Foundation in the deep snow of winter, a stark contrast to the abundance of greens that she would later come to know of the summer months. Located on the south side of Chicago, on the edge of a neighborhood called Englewood, once a thriving black community but now known for all the wrong reasons and heavily surveilled by the Chicago Police department. The writing on the pavement crossroads demarcates territory laid out by local gangs, undetected by some and clearly read by others. Here, a hand-raised barn sits in the middle of a snowy field, across the road from the small street which divides an active wood workshop and a previously foreclosed house, now reactivated—now a spatialization of pedagogy. Clad with polycarbonate, the Thought Barn is a space for the community to gather, eat together, and engage in cultural activity. The Barn is adorned with the recognizable Chicago flag, usually endowed with only four stars—reminders of four significant events in the history and formation of the city. But this flag has a fifth. The additional star, bears witness to the Great Migration of African Americans in search of better prospects than the abusive Jim Crow laws they were subjected to in the Deep South.

Chicago's south side—the megatropolis, the city within a city, once comprising one of the largest populations of African Americans in the States—has been in diminishing population decline over the last decade. As many migrated from the South, redlining policies determined where African-Americans were permitted to live, poor building maintenance, denial of mortgages, and the designation of areas deemed unfit for insurance, proved no less barbaric practices than what the continuously underserved communities of the South experience today. The ongoing closure of public schools, destruction of public housing, and lack of amenities have created a climate of constant upheaval, displacement, and dispersal in what was once a thriving black community.

As she enters the workshop, the smell of sawdust surrounded the team of carpenters, some more youthful and than the more experienced Big Mike, all busy cutting and sanding wood. The atmosphere is alive with conversation and laughter, as well as the song of a man called Rudy reminiscing about what he refers to as "the classics." The program offers an opportunity for apprenticeship in woodwork, beginning with learning how to build a small seat.

As she leaves the workshop, a large manifesto reads "We the Publics" signals to a "we" and lists various publics formed through space, architecture, and education leaves space for new additions.

She climbs the small stoop at the back of the house that looks over the vegetable garden, with a sign overhead carved into a small piece of wood. The 'Think-Do House' because, if you can think it, draw it and plan it properly, you can do it, she is later told. She is introduced to Mama Betty, a woman perhaps in her late fifties wrapped from head to toe in West African prints. Mama Betty is preparing macaroni and cheese, chicken, and collard greens for the workers in the kitchen at the back of the house. A large jug of sweet tea sits on the counter. She fist bumps Mama Betty while complimenting the hunger-inducing aromas as she continues to the dining hall. At the end of the dining hall, two women sit typing at their computers. They are surrounded by walls painted in blackboard paint and covered in chalk writing. This is a pedagogical space, a community school, a place to eat, meet, and greet.

The Amtrak railway lies opposite the house, with occasional double-decker trains passing by. This house she stands in now was raised to speculate on the land previously occupied by row houses, which were deemed unfit for living and torn down. Colorful photos of the Sweet Water Foundation throughout the summer months, the months of harvest, adorn the walls, along with a poster displaying definition of the word "radical:" "Of or pertaining to the root." Emmanuel says that if you want to be radical you have to reach below the surface of the ground to the root. To rebuild this community we needed to restitute the land. Emmanuel explains that while "blight" is a word often used to describe an urban condition, it is actually an agrarian term. Through reestablishing a relationship with the land, Sweet Water Foundation has begun to create a set of relationships that reclaim the land as a commons, by growing the neighborhood through pedagogy. This incoming community is not one that speculates on land and sees it purely as capital gain but recognizes the social and spatial value of pedagogy and agriculture.

"There grows the Neighbourhood."

Emmanuel Pratt, *There Grows the Neighborhood*, Sweet Water Foundation, Chicago, Illinois.

Sepake Angiama is the artistic director of the Institute for International Visual Arts (Iniva) in London, which is home to the Stuart Hall Library. Sepake served as co-curator of Chicago Architecture Biennial and is the initiator of Under the Mango Tree, a self-organized gathering of decolonizing and unlearning practices. She has also held positions at the Hayward Gallery, London, Turner Contemporary, Margate, the International Foundation Manifesta, The Netherlands, and documenta 14, Greece and Germany.

FLOOR TABLE AND ARCHITECTURE OF INTERVALS

The floor table is where people gather for meals in Anatolian tradition. Food is served in communal plates; a large round table or tray is placed on a piece of cloth, and people sit around it in a circle. The table is usually raised about twenty to thirty centimeters above the floor, where people are seated. Hands and spoons reach across the floor table to taste a morsel of food.

Modernization meant a transformation of the table from the floor to a raised position, with people seated on chairs, served in individual plates, and using cutlery. The host typically sits at the head of the table, and good citizens are taught how to sit and eat at the table. Nation-state officials sit down together at the modern table to serve as examples for modern society. In this process, the floor table was discarded, and its not-so-good users excluded. Yet recently, new state officials have reappropriated the floor table to display the importance of preserving traditional values, this time excluding those sitting at the modern table from good citizenship, and destroying the possibility of gathering, once again.

Interested in possibilities for gathering outside of the politics that have occupied people's everyday lives, dividing, segregating, and alienating them, I want to discuss how Matbakh-Mutfak—a women's collective in Gaziantep, Turkey—reinterprets the floor table in the context of an architecture of intervals. The collective (of which I am also a part) is composed of Turkish, Syrian, and Kurdish women, who established the kitchen collective in a very small room on the ground floor of a cultural center in Gaziantep. The floor table takes up almost the entire space, enabling women to sit around it, prepare meals, and eat all together, while having conversations and producing new ideas. In this context, there are two aspects of the floor table to focus on:

1. An Architecture of Intervals
This refers to the proximity between two things (subjects, beings, people, situations, formations, etc.) that may seem far away from each other. The circular floor table, which is closed to the ground and shared by several people, constitutes an architecture of equal intervals. The interval describes the space between any two people around the table, but also the distance between the center and the periphery of the circle. Yet it also potentially relates to those who are far away, and to the possibility of togetherness.

2. A Principle of Participation

The women in the collective participate in decision-making, while also sharing space around the same floor table. The idea of "cityzenship"—being from the same city—which is acknowledged by municipal law and greatly contributes to the principle of participation, is taken up by the kitchen collective, around the floor table.

Merve Bedir is an architect, based in Hong Kong. Her work focuses on hospitality and commoning practices in the context of mobility and labor. Merve is an Adjunct Assistant Professor in Hong Kong University. She is the co-founder of Land and Civilization Compositions and Aformal Academy (Shenzhen/Hong Kong), and a founding member of the Center for Spatial Justice (Istanbul), and the Mutfak مطبخ Workshop (Gaziantep).

Freeing the subject's position and point of view from relative convictions is only possible by rethinking these dynamics, which are not only embedded in the subject but in the totality of existence/subsistence. We all live in the same city. Locating and reproducing our subjectivities around the floor table opens up the possibility of gathering to emerge, not only for women but for all.

Sini floor table, 1966. Copper, 85 cm diameter.

Turgut Zaim, *Yörükler Köyü*, 1964. Oil painting, 17.5 × 99.5 cm.

FATTOUSH
BAR GALLERY:
MODERNITY
REUSED

ALONA NITZAN-SHIFTAN

The generous space of Fattoush Bar & Gallery is packed with spectacular and eclectic reused objects, and offers a Middle Eastern feast of visual arts, music, cuisines, and spirits that criss-cross the historic subdivisions of the region. This resurgence of Palestinian culture in Haifa is remarkably recent and astonishingly challenging in a city that, until the 1948 war, had been evenly coinhabited by Arabs and Jews. Fattoush Bar & Gallery soberly and unapologetically engages this by locating its premises exactly at the crossroads of the divided histories it negotiates. The exuberant eclecticism of its interior space, its porous urban context, and its proximity to modern infrastructures, comfortably weave in the different periods, sovereigns, economies, and mobilities that typified modernity in the Middle East. The vibrant intimacy of the used objects eases the encounter with the ideological newness and the dramatic ruptures that this modernity inflicted upon Haifa.

Cultural entrepreneur Wadie Shahbarat and K.O.T Architects curated spatial and material relationships and engaged with modern histories more than simply by constructing a space. Their 1940s warehouse was built on a newly claimed land in Haifa's port. It was designed by Robert Friedmann—a Jewish architect who fled Hamburg with the rise of Nazism, and owned by Mann&Berman Ltd., a firm that no longer exists. Shahbarat and K.O.T Architects scoured Haifa's flea markets and auctions for renovation materials, collecting doors, windows, loading slabs, and iron handrails from different geographies and periods. They also collected couches, paintings, Arab calligraphy, packed vitrines, Disney figures, naval projectors, and soft Tiffany-inspired lamps that, when placed together in the unique space, form "a cabinet of curiosities" of sorts—an assemblage striking the senses with a feast of colors and textures and lights. The Levantine modernity this setting evokes and even celebrates is not only of progress and novelty, but also of trade, transfer, migration, and chasms between incompatible realities.

Outside, this encounter assumes urban dimensions. The British-era port, naval center, railroad hub, and oil terminal form the northern border of Fattoush's outdoor space; fast trains partake in the bustling activity at the bar, and cranes make up an industrial background. The UN Partition Plan, the war it ignited, and the Israeli destruction of the Ottoman downtown are also

ALONA NITZAN-SHIFTAN

visible and present in the derelict abandoned lots and the curated graffiti surrounding the compound. Bold government office towers complete the juxtaposition, anchor Israeli statehood, and conclude the panorama of entangled Ottoman, British, Palestinian, and Israeli histories.

What, then, does Fattoush represent? How does it host movies and music from the Arab world—unapologetically omitting Hebrew from its publicity—while enjoy an ever-growing popular reception amongst the Hebrew-speaking majority of this town? Perhaps Fattoush won critical acclaim exactly because it inhabits Haifa's ruptured modernity without succumbing to the almost knee-jerk reaction to conjure a possible future of healing when faced with a complex, and often brutal, past. Or perhaps it is because Fattoush argumentatively strips modernity from its mantle of exclusive newness, its notion of frontier, and treats it simply as what we have. Through its used, familiar items, Fattoush introduces a rare intimacy into these troubled histories, and identifies them not only with pain, but also with an exuberance and joy that open up a space where people can experience together separate histories.

Alona Nitzan-Shiftan is an architectural historian and theorist, and an Associate Professor at the Technion. She heads the Arenson Built Heritage Research Center, where she works on the politics of architecture and heritage. Her awarded book *Seizing Jerusalem: The Architectures of Unilateral Unification* will be followed by the Israeli volume of *Modern Architectures in History* (Reaktion Books).

ALONA NITZAN-SHIFTAN

K.O.T Architects and Planner,
Fattoush Bar Gallery, interior.

SHE: *ALAE AND NATHALIE*

As a Lebanese-born American artist and mother, my cross-cultural experiences inform my art. I have dedicated my work to exploring issues of personal and collective identity through photographs of female adolescence and woman-hood—both in the United States, where I live, and in the Middle East, where I am from. I am interested in what it means to be a girl and a woman in a world that poses endless questions of girls and women of all backgrounds.

My work addresses states of "becoming"—the fraught beauty and the vulnerability of growing up—in the context of our visceral relationships to our physical environment and universal humanity. It is also about collaboration, experimentation, performance, empowerment, and pushing the limits of creativity and self-expression—both for the young women I work with and for myself.

I have recently started collaborating with two twenty-year-old women who seemingly had nothing in common between each other: Alae, a Shia Muslim woman from Southern Lebanon, and Nathalie, a Jewish woman from Weston, Massachusetts. Whereas their lives and backgrounds are very different, they are both college students at similar stages of their young lives and are alike in more ways than one could imagine, especially in their love of art and the artistic process. Our collaboration became regular and intense, and extended to different locations and seasons, with each bringing her own creativity to the process. I eventually found myself developing a similar and parallel collaborative relationship with each of them, and introduced them virtually to each other on Instagram. They instantly connected and we started a back-and-forth collaborative artistic relationship across continents, which coincided with my own trips between Lebanon and the United States. Each photographic encounter with one would elicit a photographic response from the other and so on, as I shared the images with them and acted as the visual "messenger."

By collaborating with these two young women, one in the United States and one in the Middle East, I am focusing on our essence, our physicality, and the commonalities that make us human, ultimately highlighting how female subjectivity develops in parallel forms across cultural lines. In the

Rania Matar was born and raised in Lebanon and moved to the US in 1984. Matar received a 2018 Guggenheim Fellowship, 2017 Mellon Foundation artist-in-residency grant, 2011 Legacy Award at the Griffin Museum of Photography, and 2011 and 2007 Massachusetts Cultural Council artist fellowships. She has published four books: *SHE* (Radius Books, 2021), *L'Enfant-Femme* (Damiani Editore, 2016), *A Girl and Her Room* (Umbrage Editions, 2012), and *Ordinary Lives* (Quantuck Lane Press, 2009). She is associate professor of photography at the Massachusetts College of Art and Design.

divisive world we live in today, I hope that these images and this unlikely collaboration between two beautiful young women of very different backgrounds can reveal the delicate and multilayered beauty in our shared humanity—in the universal as well as personal experience of young women encountering the challenges of growing up regardless of background, culture, and religion.

Rania Matar, *Alae, Khivam, Lebanon*, 2019.

Rania Matar, *Nathalie, Weston, Massachusetts, United States*, 2019.

INCLUSIVE
CREATIVITY

Good architecture happens in much the same way that good communities evolve: celebrating shared traditions, confronting mutual difficulties, protecting people from hazards, conjuring up collective visions for the future. The process often breaks but then it keeps going, largely because it is so inclusive. Architectural collaboration can likewise engage myriad participants. The clients go far beyond those who commission a project to include all sorts of ordinary individuals who are essential to how a building functions and what it means. These are the people who help enliven spaces and resolve conflicts so we can live together.

Architects often presume that they intuitively know what other people want and how they will act. This myopia can be limiting and even dangerous. Creative talent is no substitute for close attention to the needs, desires and difficulties of particular groups, especially vulnerable populations like children, the elderly, minorities and immigrants, and the mentally or physically disabled, for example. Astute and knowledgeable individuals who are attuned to specific risks can help us avoid them—and discover new possibilities in the process. In *The Public and its Problems* (1927), John Dewey called on all professionals to create what he called "constituted communities" that extend beyond their peers, continually expanding to include more diverse and challenging voices.

Koning Eizenberg Architecture (KEA) embodies this open-minded, upbeat and savvy attitude about the design process. Hank Koning and Julie Eizenberg's firm takes in many kinds of ideas and insights about each new building and its surroundings. This includes lots of informal exchanges as well as highly focused research on environmental issues, local history, and social equity. Far from stifling creativity, this approach makes for buildings that resonate like exhilarating modern music, even as they nurture a community. Recognizing that architects "facilitate rather than control the action," KEA's 2006 book, *Architecture Isn't Just for Special Occasions,* boldly declares: "We like the ad hoc, the discovered, the legitimization of the unexpected."[1] Fittingly, the book opens with full-page color photos of individual users from six of the firm's projects, alongside pithy statements about something each person had said they hoped would happen with the new building.

The ability to listen well requires both curiosity and a patience for close but wide-ranging observation. It is much like a good doctor's diagnosis, extending from the minutiae of one person's condition to the collective public health. The benefits are exponential. Showing people respect encourages them to take an active part in the process of healing—and the creation of successful places.

Creativity is not autonomous; it encompasses a deep empathy for people, an attentive eye for detail, finely honed research, flashes of brilliant innovation and ongoing improvisations, led by architects but implemented and adapted by many others. Since the local context is always important, Koning Eizenberg's base in Santa Monica, California, can remind us that the process of architecture should also be fun: We can be like surfers who learn to enjoy riding powerful waves, always cognizant that it is treacherous to fear or ignore their force.

Gwendolyn Wright is now a Professor Emerita at Columbia University's GSAPP. Her most recent book is *USA*, part of the *Modern Architectures in History* series from Reaktion Books. For ten years she was also a host of the PBS television series, *History Detectives*.

Koning Eizenberg Architecture,
28th Street Apartments,
Los Angeles, California, 2012.

1   Koning Eizenberg Architecture, *Architecture Isn't Just for Special Occasions: Koning Eizenberg Architecture* (New York: The Monacelli Press, 2006), 32.

BEYOND THE NEO-WEGO: STUDIO-MLA

AMY MURPHY

The year is 2020. The location is Downtown Los Angeles. That is about as futuristic sounding a description as any Hollywood screenwriter might conjure.

Yet, if we were to trust recent depictions of this city in the cinema to answer the question of how will we live together, the resounding response would be: "Not very well." Even prior to the exacerbating experience of alienation and fear brought on by the current global pandemic, long-standing anxiety about lack of resources combined with an abundance of poorly-served humanity undercut our ability to imagine a future Los Angeles where the needs of the collective can be adequately balanced with the desires of individuals. More often than not, any narrative resolution provided for in futuristic or post-apocalyptic films is reactionary rather than progressive—advocating the return of society to smaller eusocial units (or clans), away from the urban core. In the most conservative of these narratives, each apocalyptic event is seen as providing a form of ethnic cleansing, a means to an end, after which a chosen few can return to an idealized, segregated past to begin again.

In contradiction to these bleak visions of the future, there are architects and landscape architects working today in a quite different direction towards a more equitable, inclusive future Los Angeles—specifically, landscape architect Mia Lehrer and her office, Studio-MLA. Over the past thirty years, Lehrer has produced numerous transformative projects throughout the region, including Vista Hermosa Park, Franklin Ivar Park, the Natural History Museum of Los Angeles Nature Gardens, and most recently, the First and Broadway Park (in collaboration with OMA), to name a few. Together, these projects have begun to form a network to support the future Los Angeles by synergizing the overlapping interests of our communities and ecological systems. With most located in former industrial zones around the edges of Downtown, these projects do not just provide "parks" or "green spaces" for the nearby residents, but actively work to reverse a century of injustice and neglect. Nature, as well as the often-hidden communities surrounding these projects, are now imagined by Lehrer as essential to creating a vibrant future city "for all"—rather than remaining exploitable resources serving the few.

Ultimately, the answer to the question of how will we live together depends on the definition of "we." As any typical post-apocalyptic film illustrates, the greater the lack of resources, the more the "we" stands for fewer and fewer people. During the latter part of the eighteenth century, a period of time with significant social and political upheavals not unlike today, the use of the term "we" reached an unprecedented level in public rhetoric. In addition to producing the phrase "we the people" (which of course did not then include *all the people*), this era added the word "wegotism" to our vocabulary, as a conjunction of "we" plus "egotism," to define the habit of referring to oneself with the collective pronoun "we."

Unlike this common misuse of the term "we" (to actually mean a slightly larger "me"), Mia Lehrer's work in Los Angeles advocates for a much more complex and necessary "we"—a "we" that includes not only all of us who live in this city today, but also the city's future generations and ecologies as well.

Amy Murphy is an Associate Professor at University of Southern California School of Architecture. She has published several pieces examining apocalyptic thought in cinema, including "The Future Tradition of Nature," "New Orleans, Nature and the Apocalyptic Trope," and "Nothing Like New: Our Post-Apocalyptic Imagination as Utopian Desire." Currently, Amy is completing a new manuscript entitled *After the Symphony: Cinematic Representation of the American City 1939–1989.*

Studio-MLA, *LA River Revitalization Plan.*

Studio-MLA, *Natural History Museum.*

CONNECTED
APART

How do we take on the existential crises of our world—climate change, migration, social and economic inequity, the rise of nationalism—when the lure of the ever-updating virtual world is continually eclipsing physical reality? How will we live together under this condition?

A quarter century ago, in 1994, Mark C. Taylor, a professor of religion and philosophy, coined the term "electrotecture" to identify a new kind of space where communities would develop, a space that architecture would need to explore, consider, and help to shape. Since then, these communities have been largely developed by computer coders and engineers. We do not know if the so-called online spaces of Google, Facebook, Amazon, or Alibaba would be different, or better, if architects had in some way given them form. But without question, in the future we will live together online, because regardless of what one calls home, we already do.

In 2020, an estimated 2.87 billion people around the world will have smartphones in their pockets, handheld lifelines that require only an electrical infrastructure to maintain—something as simple as the new digital sign kiosks in Manhattan, where the homeless, too, recharge their smartphones (which are easier to access than housing). Holding a phone, swiping left or right, and texting, one meets people online. Architect Andrés Jaque of the Office for Political Innovation notes the demise of the gay night-club to the Grindr app—what he calls "Grindr urbanism"—which allows men to meet in private rather than public places. It is no longer atypical for wedding announcements in the *New York Times* to say that couples, gay and straight, met through dating apps. Naturally, the space of the bed figures in these scenarios, but architectural historian and theorist Beatriz Colomina posits that the bed has also become a workspace. With WiFi, a smartphone, and a laptop, the bed is a Zoom office, a Doordash dining room, and a Netflix movie theater—work, living, and entertainment spaces shaped by software. Kalle Lasn, an activist and founding editor of *Adbusters*, sees the smartphone as a revolutionary tool that governments and corporations already use to win elections and enhance their brands. And the public agoras of Reddit and Twitter have overturned architecture's socio-spatial contract through scrolling feeds and hashtags that are changing ideas of space and language.

Living online doesn't eliminate physical space, though it may shape it. Investors now see opportunity in eSports arenas for the estimated 380 million video gamers in the US and Europe. Populous, a sports architecture firm, is designing screen-clad arenas with multiple points of sale for fans to gather and watch gamer competitions, tapping a revenue stream that *Building Design + Construction* reports could hit one billion dollars this year. A 2017 gaming tournament in Katowice, Poland, drew an astonishing 173,000 fans to a multiuse stadium—but forty-six million more watched online.

"While electricity concentrates, electronics disperse," Taylor wrote in *ANY* Magazine in 1994. Cyberspace can be isolating, but it also gives peripheral communities and individuals who have had difficulty being heard or navigating the physical world new ways to interact and feel connected.

The world needs more spaces for beds, but the spaces of art galleries, karaoke bars, and classrooms, alongside social networks like Instagram and sites like WebMD, are accessible to every population via smartphones, despite nationalism. After the COVID-19 pandemic, no one will willingly give up these potentially resilient connections.

Cynthia Davidson is editor of the journal *Log* and the Writing Architecture Series books at MIT Press, and executive director of the nonprofit Anyone Corporation architecture think tank in New York City. She never expected to be teaching, talking, and meeting online this past year.

Lesley Lokko and Beatriz Colomina, Dutch Pavilion *WORK, BODY, LEISURE*, 16th International Architecture Exhibition, La Biennale di Venezia, *FREESPACE*, 2018.

Andrés Jacque/Office for Political Innovation, *Intimate Strangers*, 2016.

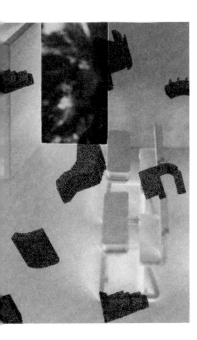

AS (IN)
DEPENDENT
AS POSSIBLE
ON/OF
EACH
OTHER

Dear A.,

It's nice to hear from you. I do not know how all this time has passed. Curfews and project cancellations/rescheduling presented us with other purposes and projects for our time. I am rewriting my piece, as I have recently been brought on board of a project that involves building a community of ideas.

This community's main idea is to develop a model for a school on a 1,000 sqm plot of land that could be/move anywhere. On this land, we imagine active engagement in/of networks, ideas, education, tools, and models of exchange within creative networks.

Our initial site is part of a larger, 50,000 sqm terrain in Jordan. It is an agricultural land, which was secured through a ten-year agreement wherein land is given for free and gets developed in return. On 1,000 sqm we want to envisage a school—a safe, productive space surrounded by a cultivated land expanse. We imagine it as a creative school, inclusive of people with (dis)abilities; it will not only teach arts and music, it will also crucially incorporate them within teachings of the compulsory national curriculum. The aim is to build one class a year. Each grade is a school. In ten years, we will have ten schools, but each school is a model, it has only one room. By the third year, we want to expand vertically. I am asking my Japanese architect friends to help us design this model that can grow/move/be built in any direction. The vertical growth will allow us to utilize the surrounding land for farming and land experiments: we are thinking about and through land that we do not own but can use, and want to offer our community (of program leaders as much as of students) the chance to work and produce, thus providing income by/to the students. You tell me that over 85% of children with disabilities do not attend schools, and moreover, they often do not find a productive place for them within society. This school includes, empowers, and integrates less-socially-integrated individual talents and provides them with learning and work opportunities in and outside of school.

How do we imagine a project dependent on land, yet where movability is crucial to its concept? It is the way we carry our architecture with us is that is essential here; not just in the processes of (un)building and (un)learning but also in arriving to social acceptance of who our community is made of. It is in such interrogations that filmmaker Jean-Luc Godard found himself speaking through drawings to fighters about the film he was planning about them; it took him/them five more years to realize that this communication was about resetting his and their relationship to the systems that mobilize, produce, and define/design us. In addition to fighters, he relates this liberation to farmers and the young future-inheritors of this effort, and to the performativity of its launch. In the following quote, we see eyes that survey, lips that inform, arms that pick up, backs that bend, and ears that identify the sound of what is going to change.

Ala Younis is an artist with research, curatorial, film, and publishing projects. Younis's projects are expanded experiences relating to materials from distant times and places. She is a member of the Advisory Board of Berlinale's Forum Expanded the Akademie der Künste der Welt in Cologne. She co-founded Kayfa ta, a non-profit publishing initiative that publishes in book and exhibition formats.

"The people's army does not consist of sophisticated radars. They are 10.000 children with binoculars and walkie-talkies.... [The] first bullet has to be fired close to the ears of the farmers, so that they can hear the sound of liberation of the land. That is a revolutionary sound."[1]

We not only want to enhance our (precarious) ability to listen to and address carefully the distanced and less heard, the dismembered, but also to actively produce, convince, and conduct, as (in) dependently as possible on/of each other.

1   Abû Hassan, a Palestinian fida'i who published an article in the first issue of the Fedayeen bulletins, quoted in Jean-Luc Godard, "Manifeste," *El Fatah* (July 1970), published as "Jusqu'à la Victoire," trans. Stoffel Debuysere, as part of the research project Figures of Dissent: Cinema of Politics/Politics of Cinema (KASK/ University of Ghent School of Arts, 2012–2016), *Diagonal Thoughts*, November 28, 2012, https:// www.diagonalthoughts.com/?p=1728.

Ala Younis, *As (In)dependent as Possible on/of Each Other*, series of digital images, 2021.

AARON BETSKY

LIVE ARCHITECTURE: THE SCHOOL OF ARCHITECTURE AT TALIESIN AND BEYOND

Between 2015 and 2020, I had the pleasure of directing the School of Architecture at Taliesin. Founded as an apprenticeship program by Frank Lloyd Wright in 1932, the School carried forward the practice of a creative community that believes we can make a world that is more sustainable, open, and beautiful. Though the School has now been exiled from its site, there is much we can learn from its model and tradition.

The notion that a community of learning is not just an institution where you receive instruction and possibly live together, but also a collective engaged in the acquisition of the knowledge and skills proper to a discipline as well as a place where learners of all ages gather to experiment, make, and weave together a social skein is, of course, not new. Wright based the apprenticeship program on the Arts and Crafts communities of the nineteenth and early twentieth century, and in particular on the fellowship Charles Robert Ashbee founded in London in 1888. Frank Lloyd Wright brought young men and women to his office, home, and farm, which he called Taliesin, in Spring Green, Wisconsin. There, they not only worked on such design commissions as he had in the office, but also farmed, cooked, cleaned, built and repaired the buildings on the site, made music, performed, and entertained guests.

For the last forty years, the School continued that mode as an accredited graduate program in architecture. The students and some of the faculty and staff lived and worked together in both Spring Green and at the "winter camp" Wright set up in Scottsdale, Arizona, in 1937 (Taliesin West). They ate and cooked together, performed, and worked to create a community. Before each student graduated, they have to design, build, and occupy a shelter in the desert at Taliesin West, and then produce a thesis based on their experience about how we can live in our modern world.

As faculty members and administration, we believed such shelters could be prototype elements for communities that might form the basis for a critical alternative to both the mindlessness of sprawl and the wasteful agglomeration of people, goods, and services in dense, unjust, and over-scaled cities. Of particular interest to us was the question of whether we can begin to build a form of human community that is truly sustainable, not through gadgets applied to new buildings, but through an intelligent reuse and reimagination of existing structures and landscapes. Such a tactic might lead to the creation of a carpet of human-made activity that provides nodes of connection and cultural intensity within territories no longer defined in terms of either city, suburb, and exurb, or country, clan, or religion. Occupied by new nomads who move and create temporary communities depending on the flows of capital and resources, this is a pattern in which we would live light on the land in what Gordon Matta-Clark once called "anarchitecture."

As noted above, the Frank Lloyd Wright Foundation, which owns all of Wright's property, both intellectual and physical, exiled the School last year and it is now operating out of Arcosanti, a somewhat similar compound started by one of Wright's disciples, Paolo Soleri. For my part, I have taken the experiences of the School with me to Virginia Tech, where I now direct the School of Architecture + Design. A land-grant university with a strong tradition of both community service and experimentation, I believe this School is well-suited to continue the Taliesin effort within the framework of a larger institution. Check back with us in another five years.

Aaron Betsky is the Director of the School of Architecture + Design at Virginia Tech. Previously he was President of the School of Architecture at Taliesin, Director of the Cincinnati Art Museum, Director of the Netherlands Architecture Institute, and Curator of the 11th International Architecture Exhibition of La Biennale di Venezia. Trained as an architect, he is active as a critic, writer, and designer.

Nelson Schleiff, *Shelter Project* as part of thesis work at the School of Architecture at Taliesin.

Jan Sobotka, *Shelter Project* as part of thesis work at the School of Architecture at Taliesin.

STAY CONCERNED: TEN YEARS AFTER *SMALL SCALE, BIG CHANGE*

A strong divide becomes apparent within the architectural discipline when looking back on the past decade. This division mirrors a ghastly, growing economic inequality and its brutal consequences.[1] On the one hand, there are a small number of highly powerful architectural practices serving the global capital elite, with the capacity to design large-scale projects, from airports to entire cities. These offices often employ hundreds of architects, organized in hierarchical structures. They resemble major companies highly dependent on big money to fuel their system. Like these companies, their awareness of the ethical and social responsibility of their designs is rather limited. On the other hand, there exist an increasing number of small offices—sometimes comprised of just a single individual—who initiate building projects that stand for a socially-relevant, sustainable, and ethical architecture. This movement, seen in various parts of the world, has been described as the "social turn" in architecture.[2] Predecessors of this turn have existed before in the twentieth century, but a renewed engagement toward social relevance in the discipline became visible in the early 2000s. Key projects such as Francis Kéré's elementary school in Gando, Burkina Faso mark such revival. The growing wave of like-minded endeavors was a multi-local phenomenon: few personal connections existed between the key protagonists and there was no joining theory bringing them together. The turn's various representatives were united only by the strong motivation to develop a critical and ethical response to the formal excesses of "starchitecture" beginning in the 1990s. Exhibitions such as *Small Scale, Big Change: New Architectures of Social Engagement* at the Museum of Modern Art in New York in 2010 also contributed in unifying and bringing such ideas together to a broader audience. This show presented a number of highly engaged projects that aimed to reconnect the profession with the increasing global challenges of migration, rapid growth of informal settlements, and economic inequalities. Ten years later, it seems reasonable to reflect on the long-term impact of this exhibition and the optimistic atmosphere that accompanied it. Has it changed the social relevance of the discipline in general? There is no simple answer. It is encouraging to see the growing success of some architects who contributed to the exhibition since then. Francis Kéré, Anne Lacaton and Jean-Philippe Vassal, and Alejandro Aravena have all succeeded in expanding and upscaling their projects, even if their work and ideas have only limited impact on a big scale. Socially-engaged architecture has become an important niche with remarkable results and a growing public attention attracted to the energy of its groundswell. Even so, the profession has not changed its direction much overall and the gap between the most economically successful in the field and those practices trying to improve social impact seems to widen. We need to stay concerned about the aim of architecture and its relevance for our global society.

Andres Lepik started as Curator in 1994 at Neue Nationalgalerie, Berlin. From 2007 he was Curator at the Architecture and Design Department in MoMA, New York, presenting *Small Scale, Big Change. New Architectures of Social Engagement* in 2010. Since 2012 he is the Director of the Architecture Museum of the Technical University of Munich and Professor for Architecture History and Curatorial Studies.

1   Patricia Cohen, "Study Finds Global Wealth is Flowing to the Richest," *New York Times*, January 19, 2015, Section B6.

2   Anna Richter, Katharina Göbel, and Monika Grubbauer, "Designed to Improve?: The Makings, Politics, and Aesthetics of 'Social' Architecture and Design," *City* 21, no. 6 (2017): 769–778.

Kéré Architecture, *Primary School in Gando*, Burkina Faso, 2001.

BUILDING
ARGUMENTS

SARA DEYONG

We do not always think of buildings as social or political arguments about the built environment. Rather, buildings are more typically seen as manifestations of power, which architects have little say over, with regards to social and political matters. Since policy, program, zoning, code, economics, and ergonomics, determine form well before the architect has a chance to come to the table, design agency, it would seem, lies not with architects but with those higher up in the food chain: planners, policy makers, entrepreneurs, community leaders, and social activists.

And yet, contemporary studios, such as The Open Workshop, Lateral Office, UrbanLab, LCLA Office, Design Earth, and NEMESTUDIO (to name just a few), are challenging the assumption that the discipline, by virtue of its focus on building, harbors little social and political agency. In so doing, they are also challenging the stereotypical divide between academia and the profession, renegotiating the formal and sociopolitical divide within architecture itself, and making new projective arguments about our built environment that extend beyond the boundaries of the discipline proper. As Pier Vittorio Aureli points out, although The Open Workshop is critical of architecture's tendency to naturalize institutions of power through form, they also see architectural form as the medium by which agency is made manifest: "[T]heir way of producing architectural form makes evident that the source of [their] forms are architectural 'common places'—such as the linear sequence, the striation of activities, the grid, the stacking of different forms, etc. These elements are developed out of a renewed commitment to a modernist vocabulary, which The Open Workshop is not afraid to reinvigorate."[1]

Indeed, what distinguishes practices such as The Open Workshop is the presence of enduring architectural elements derived from a modernist lexicon uniquely tied to the design of buildings, while at the same time engaging other disciplinary boundaries.[2] These practices engage issues that might appear to belong to other disciplines, but in their hands, they do not. Their approach is visual, tactile, kinesthetic and spatial: in a word, architectural. When they make other domains the substance of their arguments, such as landscape, infrastructure, planning, history, art or geography, the elements of their reflective and projective statements on what is and what could be are explicitly of the discipline.

To be sure, by elements, I do not mean the standardized, component parts of a building, whose evolution is the source of new typologies, but rather the elements of an architectural composition. *Parti*, *poché*, figure-ground, dimension, arrangement, scale, grid, axis, and entourage are some of the more classic elements. To these, Alois Riegl famously added *style*; Le Corbusier, *promenade*; Colin Rowe (with Robert Slutsky), *phenomenal transparency*; and Nigel Coates and Bernard Tschumi, *narrative*. More recently, Robert Somol has added *shape* to the lexicon; Andrew Kovacs and Mark Foster Gage, *kit-bashing*; and Dora Epstein Jones, *populated plans*. Every culture, moreover, has their own translation of these terms, which can be highly specific to their histories and contexts.

These irreducible elements are the stuff of every architectural argument worth its weight in salt—irreducible in the "triple o" sense that their meanings can never be exhausted.[3] Although their meanings may change over time, and the contexts in which they are translated and deployed are endless, there is something about them that we implicitly recognize *as* architecture. Architects who make polemical arguments and take positions rarely spend time explaining their design process to their audiences (we have critics who do that work), for the elements have no particular agency in and of themselves. They do not constitute positions in and of themselves. It is *how* they are actualized into content and mobilized in different contexts that matter when it comes to the question of social and political agency, of how we will live together. As such, they are the substrate of architectural arguments, derived from the practice of designing buildings, elevated to an art.

Sarah Deyong is an Associate Professor at the University of Nebraska-Lincoln, where she previously served as program director. She has published in numerous peer-reviewed journals, conference proceedings, and books. Her essay, "The Legacy of the Sixties: Pliny Fisk's Political Ecology," garnered an ACSA/JAE Best Scholarship of Design Award. Her current pedagogical research attempts to bring greater transparency to the design process by focusing on how an architectural lexicon can be deployed to make arguments.

The Open Workshop,
*Environment as Politics:
Life Along the Conduit
During the Anthropocene,
Dredgescaping Toledo.*

162

1   Pier Vitorrio Aureli, foreword to *New Investigations in Collective Form: The Open Workshop*, ed. Neeraj Bhatia (New York: Actar; San Francisco, CA: CCA Architecture Books, 2019), 9.

2   "Embedded in the methodology," explain Lateral Office of their own approach, "is an argument for expanding fields and modes of research for architects, so they may consider buildings as just one outcome." Lola Sheppard and Mason White, preface to *Many Norths: Spatial Practice in a Polar Territory* (New York: Actar, 2017), ii.

3   OOO is the irreducibility of objects to their relations. Objects are non-relational; they resist reduction to their components or their outward effects. And yet, Graham Harman talks about changeable essences, building in part on Aristotle's notion of substance. Harman writes: "The elements [are] what cannot be broken down: The power of any world lies in its elements. Whether they're letters of the alphabet or the ingredients in a tea recipe, elements are things to conjure with. Every domain of our lives, from the nursery to the factory to the laboratory, has its recurring forms and stock characters. Once we have mastered these familiar shapes, we feel ourselves to be citizens of that kingdom." Harman, "Elements or Ether," in "Object-Oriented Philosophy: A Graham Harman Dictionary of Concepts," *Avoiding the Void* (blog), accessed October 17, 2019, https://avoidingthe void.wordpress.com/dictionary-of-concepts-for -graham-harmans-object-oriented-philosophy -draft-work-in-progress/.

SHAPING SITE AND FORMING COMMUNITY: REFLECTIONS ON THE SECOND LAGOS BIENNIAL OF CONTEMPORARY ART

The second edition of the Lagos Biennial, titled *How to Build a Lagoon with Just a Bottle of Wine?*, brought together artworks and architectural projects by forty-two individuals and collectives working in a range of mediums. Inspired by the writing of Nigerian poet Akeem Lasisi, the title speaks partly to how societies, especially in the Global South, are able to mobilize vernacular knowledge and skills in order to realize meaningfully ambitious creative and social projects despite inadequate economic resources and state support. The Biennial's overarching focus on urbanism and the built environment gave way to numerous thematic concerns, including questions about art's capacity to rejuvenate architectural sites and catalyze the formation of new communities.

Just as the Biennial's inaugural edition was sited at a decommissioned railway station on Lagos' mainland, the second edition also engaged a neglected architectural site in the city—Independence House. This dilapidated federal government building was erected in the early 1960s in the heart of Lagos Island, and today is part of Tafawa Balewa Square, which was the site of the country's independence celebrations in 1960. The curatorial team (Antawan I. Byrd, Oyindamola Fakeye, and myself) selected the building because its historical significance and its imposing scale as a twenty-five-story reinforced-concrete building made it conducive to displaying ambitious artworks.

Lagos is a city of resilience that forever evolves and adapts to a charade of constraints. The making of exhibitions in Lagos requires precisely this sense of agility. With no running water, electricity, or infrastructural resources, rejuvenating the building required the development of a micro-community for support. As the only architect on the curatorial team, I was instrumental in developing plans for renovating the four floors (30,000 square feet) and carrying out negotiations with the site's administrators. This experience called to mind the pidgin English saying, *I no come Lagos count Bridge.* This essentially means that Lagos, the city with the most advanced city infrastructure of bridges in West Africa, is the land of prosperity; against all odds, things happen in Lagos and dreams are realized.

As a megacity, Lagos has had one of the largest rural-urban migration rates in the world at 18.6% in a two-year period.[1] Without adequate housing, many immigrants end up in illegal settlements or abandoned buildings such as Independence House. The building's refurbishment and the installation process would not have been possible without the support of these squatters. Though initially cautious, we engaged squatters at Independence House with the realization that we had common goals of coexisting—living together in ways that were mutually beneficial and productive.

One of the many residents at the site who was instrumental to our success was Mr. Ben Abuze, who we hired to assist in cleaning, painting, and securing the site. Mr. Abuze is from the neighboring country of Benin; he speaks fluent English, French, and Yoruba, and is a trained painter. He also became our link to the wider community of residents in and near the building. In between the numerous challenges of delivering an event unfamiliar to its host environment, the many volunteers who offered their time did so for the opportunity to lend their voices to a cause. The Biennial was a glimpse into the "audacity of legacy" and the opportunity to enrich another generation to imagine the seemingly impossible, as suggested by the Biennial's title, *How to Build a Lagoon With Just a Bottle of Wine?*

Tosin Oshinowo is a leading architect based in Lagos, Nigeria, as well as a designer, and creative entrepreneur. Oshinowo runs cmDesign Atelier, an architecture design practice known for environmentally conscious contemporary architecture across the African Continent. Oshinowo featured on TEDx, speaking on "The Identity of an African Building." Her work in the public space of Lagos includes bringing art and design installations to the city in addition to co-curating the 2019 Lagos Biennial.

Pedro Pires, *Invisibility Container*, 2019.

Curators and community, Antawan I. Byrd, Oyindamola Fakeye, Tosin Oshinowo, Ben Abuze, 2019.

Second floor exhibition view, Lagos Biennial 2019. Straight ahead: HTL Africa, *Miracle Room*. Right: Sobelo Mlangeni, *The Royal House of Allure*.

1   Ayo Okulaja, "Lagos Leads in Global Urban Migration, According to Facebook," FutureLagos, Our Future Cities, June 18, 2014, http://futurecapetown.com/2014/06/facebook-reveals-lagos-leads-global-urban-migration/#.U6KLTZSSxYQ.

A NEW
CIRCADIA

Is it time to put architecture to sleep?

Popular culture's recent focus on sleep tells us that the biology of our well-being presumes being at rest during at least one-third of our lives. But today, the inexorable mechanization of contemporary life has evolved such that we now imagine, or even pursue, living as fully conscious, productive beings, plugged-in 24/7. The reciprocity between architecture and technology underpins this pursuit of a (not-yet) fully automated state of productivity. Its history lies in the standardization of time in the 19th century, instigated by railroads and telegraphs; and the emergence of electrically illuminated cities, and climate-controlled environments in the 20th century. These phenomena are all part of the temporal architecture of modernity, which today manifests in the ubiquity of the world-wide-web, enabling the time-shifting of labor and a global gig economy.

As a profession, architecture remains devoted to adapting technologies and schedules that override our circadian rhythms; it also creates environments the facilitate long workhours and encourage sleeplessness. Acknowledging architecture's complicity in an increasingly stressful and zombie-like world, how can we counter the over-mechanization of everyday life?

As opposed to its modern focus on the manipulation of space, architecture today might pay more attention to the marking and shaping of time. The idea of the Anthropocene raises questions about the relationship between human biology and 'deep' time, urging us to attend to the ecological implications of our technological turn. The need—and right—to idle, reset, or reject the clocks that organize our lives is an important dimension of this struggle.

Whether in the form of sleeping, dreaming, napping, lingering, or meditating, idling is not wasted time, but a state of mind and body vital to our survival and evolution as species. Our relationship to time, in any of its geological, mythical, mechanical, historical, or biological manifestations, is cultural in nature, and could be better-framed by architecture. Architecture has the capacity to organize the activities that characterize our lives—work, travel, rest, eat, pray, study, recreation, sex—even animating them in ways that challenge the sometimes-ossified types that contain them—city, office, house, bedroom, kitchen, garden, lecture-theatre, dormitory, gym. But where can we idle, without any explicit program, together?

Alluding to historical utopias (*New Atlantis, New Harmony, etc.*), *New Circadia* addresses a gap in architecture's overlooked temporal dimensions, turning attention away from a Westernized focus on isolated, sleeping individuals towards an architecture of public rest and idling. Inspired by the ancient Greek *abaton* (a proto-hospital dedicated to healing through sleep cures and collective dream incubation), and informed by Dr. Nathaniel Kleitman's Mammoth Cave Experiment (the first staging of a scientific laboratory to study human cycles of sleep and wakefulness, 1938), New Circadia's first iteration, *Adventures in Mental Spelunking* (2019–2020) was developed in collaboration with Natalie Fizer and Emily Stevenson of *Pillow Culture* (NYC). This installation conjured a primordial cave envisioned as a 'soft utopia' within a subterranean gallery at the University of Toronto. Entering through an anteroom, visitors donned specially-designed soft 'mental spelunking' gear, and proceeded to a darkened, multisensory space filled with large, sensuous, felt-covered rock-like formations. *Adventures in Mental Spelunking* integrated responsive sound, lighting, and an Oneiroi (dream capture) space. A future, mobile *Camp New Circadia* is now being planned—a proto-community engaged in activities (such as Matthew Spellberg's *Dream Parliaments*), staged within a series of liminal landscapes, all in the pursuit of collective adventure, relaxation, and reverie.

Richard Sommer is an architect, Director of the *Global Cities Institute*, and a Professor at the University of Toronto, where he recently served two terms as Dean of the Daniels Faculty. His projects and writings on urbanism, the monument, and time-based architecture include "Glossary of Dream Architecture" (*Cabinet Magazine*, 2020) and "The Democratic Monument: The Reframing of History as Heritage" (*Commemoration and the American City*, 2013).

New Circadia, *Adventures in Mental Spelunking: Softscape Cave Cove*, University of Toronto, 2019–2020

New Circadia, *Adventures in Mental Spelunking: Softscape Cave Floor*, University of Toronto, 2019–2020.

ARCHITECTURES OF SPACE AND SPIRIT: EXPANDING THE SPATIAL CONTRACT WITHIN THE WHITE CUBE

For the artist or curator, the *white cube* can be both a supposedly neutral space where architecture is invoked in service of art, or a frustrating example of an enduring and problematic mechanism of twentieth-century museum and gallery display strategies. Entering an austere and usually windowless white-walled gallery, one is enveloped in an intellectual and aesthetic landscape that focuses attention on the visual and conceptual resonance of the object of art. The modern gallery foregrounds Western ideas of space as an intellectual and conceptual project, which often excludes other cultural and intra-phenomenological experiences.

In the twenty-first century, the white cube presents another set of problematics with regard to our current social, cultural, and political landscapes. As Brian O'Doherty has argued, the modernist gallery, like a library or church, is intended not to disturb the private, individual experience of the spectator or the sanctity of art.[1] While this social and spatial contract prevails, we are seeing other examples in what the *white cube* can hold.

Models for museum tours, curatorial interventions, and commentary initiated much earlier by artists like Andrea Fraser have given way to novel acts of delivering artist talks that continue to dismantle the fourth wall between art and audience. Theaster Gates, for instance, regularly sings in a Gospel/Blues idiom to introduce himself and/or includes his musical group The Black Monks in his lectures, bringing other cultural representations and sound healing practices into the gallery.

Interdisciplinary engagements have continued to make their way into visual art spaces through dance and performance, as in Brendan Fernandes' dance-based installation *A Call and Response* in the MCA Chicago's Commons space, which invited *othered* bodies "[t]o use language, architecture and gesture... to collaborate and generate new forms of physical language."[2] Anna Martine Whitehead's project *Force,* presented at the Graham Foundation in Chicago, invited queer, trans, and gender non-conforming black, brown, and indigenous bodies to "take up space" in the foundation's gallery during a rehearsal for her dance opera created from observations and interactions between queer and trans women who meet in prison waiting rooms while visiting incarcerated loved ones."[3]

In my summer 2019 exhibition *Dark Matter: Celestial Objects as Messengers of Love in These Troubled Times,* I decided to refute the power of the white cube by painting the gallery *all black*! The space was transformed into a celestial landscape with black, glitter-covered walls, two-dozen blue and black ceramic orbs hanging from the ceiling, and a NASA video of the sun and moon looping in the gallery's catwalk above, with soundscapes by Joelle Mercedes.[4] The multisensory installation included a large, abstract, spaceship-like sculpture inspired by the vernacular architecture of a shotgun house. Together, these elements suggested an Afrofuturistic, transplanetary Middle Passage and migration through deep space. *Dark Matter* welcomed a respite from a culture troubled by unfortunate manifestations of fear, hate, greed, and a selfish disregard for others. Designer Tesh Silver's first-person review notes "… [the exhibition] invoked the theme of home, the place where we as humans belong. Home is a house, but it is also Earth, but is also the Universe."[5]

The exhibition created a safe space for intimate personal reflection, with meditation sessions and sound baths offered regularly. Perhaps there is room for an expanded spatial contract within the white cube that not only satisfies our intellectual and conceptual privileges, but also brings other cultural and spiritual practices into the mainstream.

1   Brian O'Doherty and Thomas McEvilley, *Inside the White Cube: The Ideology of the Gallery Space* (Berkeley, CA: University of California Press, 1999), 10. O'Doherty first published essays in the book in *Artforum* 14, no. 7 (March 1976). For references to the "spirit," see page 83.

2   Brendan Fernandes, *A Call and Response*, Museum of Contemporary Art, Chicago, Illinois, June 1–October 13, 2019.

3   Anna Martine Whitehead, with Seth Parker Woods and shawné michaelain holloway, *Force* (Open Rehearsal/Jam Session), Graham Foundation for Advanced Studies in the Fine Arts, Chicago, Illinois, December 14, 2019.

4   *Dark Matter: Celestial Objects as Messengers of Love* was exhibited at the Hyde Park Art Center in Chicago, Illinois, March 31–July 14, 2019. A limited edition LP exhibition catalogue will be published and distributed in early 2020 by Candor Arts, a Chicago-based publisher for the design and production of artists' books.

5   Teshika Silver, "Space is a Place: Folayemi Wilson at the Hyde Park Art Center," *Sixty Inches From Center*, November 14, 2019, http://sixtyinchesfromcenter.org/space-is-a-place-folayemi-wilson-at-the-hyde-park-art-center/.

Folayemi (Fo) Wilson is an artist/designer, educator, writer and independent curator. She is co-founder and principal of blkHaUS studios, a socially-focused design studio in Chicago, Illinois and Professor of Art & Art History at Columbia College Chicago. Her writing and reviews have appeared in *NKA, Journal of Contemporary African Art*, among other publications.

Dark Matter: Celestial Objects as Messengers of Love, Hyde Park Art Center, Chicago, 2019.

ALIVE
MUSEUM

There are two items that the interior of a museum prohibits: live plants and hot food. Despite the former's global domestication and the "parenting" that ensues from its popularity, the aliveness of plants carries the threat of infestation. Plants are food sources for pests. Following the same logic, food restrictions in museum galleries prevents an opportunity for pests—"really wild creatures"—to thrive. Museum food is permitted only with strict instructions about its consumption and given the absolute containment of its aroma. Any successful transgressions of aliveness into the museological serve to nourish pestilence—the second death of an institution and the reentry of its objects and collections into an anoxic environment.

*

Bare hands occupy the foreground of a picture. Inside a frame where color fades and vibrancy is saturated into lighter hues, the synchronicity of slim, brown hands reaching for and pinching food from a communal brass tray restores the sensuality of a space. Hand-to-mouth movement closes the gaps in the stages of eating from the mechanical grasp of fingers and the palm to the chemical processes of ingestion and digestion. The ground—an embroidered carpet and woven mat on which people are seated—realigns the focus away from the actors and subjects of looking to their unconscious coordination of the body and its organs for nutrition and pleasure. Men and women are uncannily captured chewing their food, jaws in action, and mouths filled, with a hand portioning food for the next intake. The centrality of mastication in the image pushes the wall vitrines out of the memory of this museum representation.

*

The image referent is an undated photograph of the Aga Khan Museum of Islamic Arts, the oldest and only museum dedicated to ethnic Muslims and Muslim Filipinos. Founded in 1961, the one-room repository for cultural artifacts was transferred to a building on the hills overlooking Lake Lanao thanks to an endowment from Prince Karim Aga Khan IV, who visited the city of Dansalan (now Marawi) in 1963. The non-metropolitan museum represented the local, disenfranchised Muslims in the state formation of the Philippine body politic as if it was proposing its own modernist ideas. The Aga Khan Museum has served as a general museum on the island of Mindanao: its mechanism incorporated ideas, histories, materials, and objects ranging from

RENAN LARUAN

174

across the natural sciences to daily life, until the institution's slow disintegration. Now, the museum is a field that marks the ex-corporation of bodies and identities only to be, yet again, integrated into contemporaneous narratives and discourses of conflict and disaster. The Aga Khan Museum inside the militarized zone of Marawi symbolically bleeds into the literal ground zero of the city: the perpetually preserved death (of the museum and its artifacts) expands into the more violent terrain of conquest, massacre, and demolition. Both the city and the museum form the *terra firma* of infirmities.

*

Two potted plants appear in the indoor layout of the captured museum image. Exceeding their decorative function, they could be used to scale the distances between people on the floor and the objects in the vitrines. Like our feet and hands, these plants are known carriers of soil into the museum; they conjure the image and passage of land, and ultimately, the relations that grow from it. Food and plants had entered the Aga Khan Museum. There is no other documentation that confirms their eventual departure from the building since the death of its founder in 1992. The aliveness of these plants and the conviviality of eating with bare hands in the gallery must have had introduced pests into the museum. The paradox of their presence reaffirms the diversity of other living entities.

Museums imagine themselves without pestilence: against the growth of other organisms to protect their preservation. What does it mean to reimagine the truth of a museum through the fiction of this photograph: a live museum nourishing the aliveness of all things and actions without fumigating them? With all the speech acts on opening up and decolonizing the museum, the feral potency of plants and food, this corrupted picture from Mindanao, recompose the question of pestilence: can museums grow with bare lives, with "really wild creatures" in their midst?

Renan Laru-an is the Public Engagement and Artistic Formation Coordinator of the Philippine Contemporary Art Network. He has (co-) curated the 6th Singapore Biennale (2019), *A Tripoli Agreement* (2018), the 8th OK. Video—Indonesia Media Arts Festival (2017), among others. Laru-an is a recently appointed co-curator of the 2nd Biennale Matter of Art, Prague and a Curatorial Advisor to the 58th Carnegie International.

One of the galleries of the Aga Khan Museum of Islamic Art, Marawi City, Philippines.

TIME
LANDSCAPE

PEDER ANKER

Down below our apartment on Houston Street in New York is a green space. There is nothing special about it, as it's unkempt, weedy, and inaccessible. It looks like one of those odd city spots a developer has yet to snatch up thanks to some unknown bureaucratic reason. As it turns out, the green rectangle is a thoughtful memorial to the natural world lost to architectural developments.

Time Landscape, as the plot is called, was carefully designed and built in 1978 by the artist Alan Sonfist. When he first proposed the memorial in 1965, he did so as a reaction to the construction of three high-rise buildings next to the site designed by the architect I. M. Pei. The Silver Towers, as they are named, were built by New York University with great speed between 1964 and 1966. Thanks to large scale "slum clearance" (as it was known) in the 1950s, the towers came to represent a new urban vision for New York City. They have a lucid modernist look, complete with a large Picasso statue in their courtyard. Today they are landmark buildings representing the epitome of New York modernism.

Unlike Pei and his many acolytes, Sonfist noticed the immense environmental destruction brought about by the new towers. Reflecting upon it, he decided to propose a "public monument" to the nature lost to them in analogy to "war monuments that record the life and death of soldiers."[1] With the Vietnam War raging, he saw a larger conflict taking place between modernist urbanization and natural habitat. This was a popular sentiment within the counterculture, with the Earth Day of 1970 being one of the largest demonstrations in the city's history. Other artists also began reflecting on how to think through the human vs. nature conundrum, as in the case of Walter De Maria, who created the "Earth Room" across the street in 1977.

In the late 1960s Sonfist found himself absorbed in studying the environmental history of the Silver Towers, trying to find out what the place looked like before the onslaught of urban developments. What plants did the pre-colonial environment have? How did indigenous groups in Mannahatta live? The result of his investigations came in his environmental sculpture of carefully selected trees and plants meant to capture the land and culture lost to urbanity.

Pei's modernism and Sonfist's memorial mark two opposite extremes that also frame our current architectural debates, with the most innovative designs leaning in the direction of Sonfist.

PEDER ANKER

Mitchell Joachim's butterfly sanctuary, Julia Watson's radical indigenism, and Kiel Moe's dissection of the material geography of the Seagram building may serve as examples.[2] More generally, how to avoid the pitfalls of modernism and embrace a viable environmental future is the shared challenge we face in figuring out how we will live together.

Peder Anker is Professor of History of Science and Design at the Gallatin School of Individualized Study, New York University. Recent books include *From Bauhaus to Ecohouse: A History of Ecological Design* (Louisiana State University Press, 2010), and *The Power of the Periphery: How Norway became an Environmental Pioneer for the World* (Cambridge University Press, 2020). Twitter @pederanker

1   Alan Sonfist, "Natural Phenomena as Public Monuments" (1969), in *A Companion to Public Art*, eds. Cher Krause Knight and Harriet F. Senie (Chichester, West Sussex: Wiley, 2016), 61–64.
2   See Mitchell Joachim and Maria Aiolova, *Design with Life: Biotech Architecture and Resilient Cities* (Barcelona: Actar, 2020), Julia Watson, *Lo—TEK: Design by Radical Indigenism* (Cologne: Taschen, 2020), and Kiel Moe, *Unless: The Seagram Building Construction Ecology* (Barcelona: Actar, 2021).

View of Alan Sonfist, *Time Landscape*, New York, 2019.

AN OPEN
AND
SHADED
SPACE

This last decade was marked by uprisings on the streets of major cities in the world: Arab Springs, Occupy movements in the United States and Europe, explosive revolts in Latin America, to name a few. At the same time, it was also marked by the falsification and manipulation of information, by the hacking of politics, and by a conservative turn in many countries. In Brazil the situation is no different. Major movements in the streets since 2013 have stressed important issues, such as the demand for better and more accessible public transport systems, and a greater availability of public spaces. These movements represent the outbreak of a process fermented since the previous decade with the creation of the World Social Forum and the strengthening of genuinely popular festivals, such as LGBTQ+ parades and street carnivals. All of these civil society movements, however, were accompanied by very strong conservative and moralistic reactions, which led an extreme-right candidate to assume the presidency of the Republic, dividing the country into two opposing poles. The tragic outlook of this picture, however, has nevertheless spurred important discussions about the nature and the need for public space.

Due to its colonial past and history of slavery, Brazilian society has maintained, to this date, structural features of clientelism: the habit of dealing with public affairs based on personal relationships, guided by the principle of the exchange of favors. Something that has, consequently, prevented public space from establishing itself truly as a place for everyone with the embedded potential for mediating conflicts and social differences. In the absence of this understanding, public space in Brazil is treated either as nobody's place—identified with a "them," and not with a "we," and therefore abandoned and privatized—or as a war zone, without any mediation regarding the notion of collectivity and respect for differences.

The most beautiful invention of modern Brazilian architecture is the public square sheltered by the large span of a building. An open and shaded space, qualified by the building that protects it; a merging of internal and external space, rather than an open indefinite field, like the Monumental Axis of Brasília. This paradigm was born with the Ministry of Health and Education (1936–45) in Rio de Janeiro, which frees the block for pedestrians through a square with generous pilotis. It later reached its peak with two works: the Faculty of Architecture and Urbanism of the University of São Paulo (1961–69) by Vilanova Artigas—which has hosted agitated student assemblies within its inner hall without doors—and the São Paulo Museum of Art (1957–68) by Lina Bo Bardi, with a large public space free of any structural support that is integrated into the sidewalk of the Paulista Avenue. Bo Bardi's structural effort—including pre-stressed concrete beams that support an immense freestanding space—has produced one of the most democratic public spaces in the country, a stage for important demonstrations over the last decades.

Today, bodily manifestations in public space, wherein individuals assert their identities while respecting the place of others, are the best way to resist the forms of politics that are produced, to a large extent, by the dark arena of waves of fake messages sent by WhatsApp, invisible and impervious to collective debate and the confrontation of opinions. It is in the democratic and plural public space, like MASP's free span, that we can live together while simultaneously being different.

Translated by Gabriel Kozlowski

Guilherme Wisnik is a critic, curator, and Associate Professor at the Faculty of Architecture and Urban Planning of the São Paulo State University (FAUUSP). He was Chief Curator of the 10th edition of the São Paulo Architecture Biennale (2013). His books include *Lucio Costa* (Cosac Naify, 2001), *Caetano Veloso* (Publifolha, 2005), and *Inside the Mist* (Ubu Editora, 2018).

Free and open span under the under the São Paulo Museum of Art (MASP) building, designed by Lina Bo Bardi.

Central void in the Faculty of Architecture and Urban Planning (FAUUSP) building, designed by Vilanova Artigas.

Political demonstration on Avenida Paulista occupying the MASP free span.

MICHAEL MALTZAN

...FOR A CITY OF BRIDGES...

For most of its recent life, Los Angeles (like many postwar cities) has been defined by its extraordinary physical sprawl, seemingly stretched to the horizon, unrolling into a continuity of low-slung buildings and landscapes that define its visual scene. Against this seemingly undifferentiated urban scape is a different map, made up of communities and neighborhoods largely siloed and set apart from each other. These lines of demarcation are sometimes geographic and physical, but are just as often social, political, economic—they are especially pervasive, even if they are hard to see.

These historical and enduring separations in a city like Los Angeles are increasingly being pressurized through an explosion of densification that is causing new rips and punctures in the social constructions of apartness. While these developments are positive for the long-term health and sustainability of the urban life of Los Angeles, the speed and breadth of the changes are putting enormous pressures on affordability, accessibility, mobility, and resources. In a city whose very identity was formed through the pushing outward of both its development and perimeter with a "Manifest Destiny-like" conviction, this new reality of overlaying development on the existing urban fabric is causing a self-examination of the very essence of what it means to be "Los Angeles."

Infrastructure, arguably Los Angeles' most impactful civic form, was originally meant to be the antidote for a disconnected city of distances and separations. It held the progressive promise of connection and unification through a web of democratic access for the far-flung and partitioned city. The contemporary reality is that infrastructure has now come to divide us given the collapse of easy mobility, gridlock on the highways and streets that course through the metropolis, and the literal and physical walls infrastructure creates between communities due to its relentless scale and imperviousness. Infrastructure, and its promise of connected community life has become instead a contributor to our growing disconnected and diminished civic potential.

With the extraordinary financial and physical resources we direct towards these structures, shouldn't we demand an expansion of their responsibilities beyond a purely technical and programmatic response to problems defined a generation ago, and instead ask our infrastructure to take on the deepening needs of the civic, social, and communal life of the city? Can we evolve the idea of "infrastructure" to become one of "civicstructure" and move from a "monoculture" of singular use to a "multiculture" of connection and urban vibrancy that we should expect as a culture? Perhaps the tradition of making a bridge can be a place to start.

Michael Maltzan founded Michael Maltzan Architecture, Inc. in 1995. His notable projects include the Moody Center for the Arts at Rice University, MoMA QNS, the Winnipeg Art Gallery Inuit Art Centre, the Pittman Dowell Residence, the new Sixth Street Viaduct, and MIT Vassar Street Residential Hall. His work has gained international acclaim for innovation in both design and construction.

Michael Maltzan Architecture,
Sixth Street Viaduct. 2020.

TO GATHER TOGETHER

Current situation

Master plan

185

We can live "together" by activating the verb "to gather." How do we as architects make people gather? One of the main concerns in my practice is making a place for people to build meaningful relationships that transform space into a gathering place, or what I call "placemaking."

I have been working in public spaces, using different strategies to dissolve barriers that deter people's capacity to gather and live together. Our design changes barriers into boundaries. While barriers lock everyone further into conflict, boundaries require people to communicate aspirations as well as uncomfortable issues. Designing boundaries assists in the clear expression of everyone's personal values, ultimately empowering community as a whole.

Community engagement is a key element in the activation and sustenance of public space. Public space, as we know, is an anchor for resilience and equity in society. Places bring people together and eliminate physical and mental barriers. It is up to us as architects to build trust by respecting local processes in order to build community through design. As Roland Barthes mentions in his book *How to Live Together*, "We need to recognize and respect the individual rhythms of the other," so we can collectively create new ways of living, where cohabitation does not preclude individual freedom.[1]

A new way of living together and having individual freedom is to create "common-unity." The unit (individual) and the common (collective) rearticulate the social fabric by expanding the program with actions like playing, gathering, leaning and exercising in public spaces to create a more inclusive society that empowers communities to develop identity and embrace diversity. Common-unity is common ground as well as common sense: unity within the unit.

"To do architecture without buildings," as Aaron Betsky would say, means to focus on placemaking. By creating different temporal narratives and atmospheres; rethinking space tectonically not only as closed, permanent structures, but also as open, light structures; by designing a program that enables social interaction, we rebuild society.

When users feel engaged in the design process, spatial design reshapes community relationships. For me, it is extremely important to design *with* the community and not just *for* the community through the implementation of what I call "site-actions." Site-actions are public space interventions designed to involve and gather users in creative ways that free space from preconceptions. Change begins with a shift of perception. This involves recycling and resignifying the places we design and build.

For example, the site-actions we designed for the community of Miravalle in Mexico City changed people's perception of their own space by: 1. Inviting local people to take a walk up the volcano hill nearby that allowed them to recognize their own territory; 2. Creating a path with people holding a 360 meters line of lightbulbs that highlighted a safe way to cross an insecure park or; 3. Simulating a walkway with a lime line that reactivated and integrated the site's potential to gather two disconnected neighborhoods.

Placemaking facilitates gathering, interacts through boundaries, integrates opportunity, and involves everyone's presence. The presence of all these factors is the line that connects the dots, allowing us to live together.

Rozana Montiel is a Mexican architect specialized on architectural design, artistic re-conceptualizations of space, and the public domain. The studio works on a wide variety of projects in different scales and layers that range from the city to the book, the artefact, and other micro-objects.

1 Roland Barthes, *How to Live Together: Novelistic Simulations of Some Everyday Spaces*, trans. Kate Briggs (New York: Columbia University Press, 2013), 81.

Rozana Montiel Estudio de Arquitectura, SMAQ, *Walk to the volcano*, Miravalle, Iztapalapa, Mexico, 2015.

Rozana Montiel, Tatiana Bilbao, Derek Dellekamp, Alejandro Hernández, *Walk the Line*, Miravalle, Iztapalapa, Mexico, 2016–in process.

CLOSER TO NATURE, TOGETHER

LIMIN HEE

The context of this essay is the architecture of blue and green space in Singapore, a city where water and greenery have been harnessed as part of its planning and design strategies.

Water is vital to Singapore and has offered an opportunity for a circular and sustainable approach to development. As the first country in the world to close the water loop, every drop counts in how we shape the city. Two-thirds of the island-city state is water catchment, and every drop of water is used more than once.

Since its first Tree Planting Day in 1971, Singapore has taken on the mantle of a Garden City and grown to become a City in a Garden, where greenery is not only pervasive in the city, but is an essential part of its architecture and infrastructure. The power of water and greenery lie not only in their necessity for sustenance and utility, but also in their value for urban planning, design, and climate action. Love for nature and city-building are not at odds. However, because space is a scarce resource, the narrative of a dense and green city built with nature is not just a dream, but grew out of urgent necessity.[1] Such a paradigm extends from vertical greenery at the architectural scale to the scale of a city in nature.[2]

The idea of the blue and green city enjoyed by everyone is captured within the microcosm of the Bishan-Ang Mo Kio Park and its surrounds. The Active, Beautiful, and Clean Waters Programme not only allows the city to capture and drain water, but also enables urban water to become a vital element of planning and public space.

The naturalization of drainage infrastructure creates a new public space, changing the topography of the surrounding landscape through precisely engineered solutions. The large monsoon drain has been de-concretized and the reimagined park, with its grassy banks and rolling lawns, is centered on the ensuing stream, which runs three kilometers long, with lush banks of wild flowers flanking it. Pond gardens, river plains, playgrounds, and cycling and running tracks bring the surrounding community together in this space. Its success stems not only from bringing people closer to water and nature, but from getting them to care for such spaces. The surrounding community volunteer in various ways: they create butterfly gardens, keep the waterway clean, conduct eco-life tours, grow herb gardens, and build new gravel paths.

More than 80% of Singaporeans live in public housing. In the small and densely populated island-city state, this beautiful park is not located in the city center, but between two public housing estates—it is a space for everyone, used on an everyday basis. The architectural mantle of blue and green permeates its built environment, and is a vital part of all other architectures of the city. Just as it soothes inhabitants from the tropical heat, such an architecture enriches public space, and tells the story of how we live closer to nature, together.

Limin Hee is Director of Research at Singapore's Centre for Liveable Cities, where she focuses on research strategies, content development, and international collaborations. She earlier taught at the National University of Singapore and held a teaching fellowship at the GSD Harvard University. Her recent books include *A City in Blue and Green: The Singapore Story* (Springer, 2019) and *Constructing Singapore Public Space* (Springer, 2017).

LIMIN HEE

A meandering waterway at Ang Mo Kio-Bishan Park, now a recreational space for all ages.

Before the implementation of the ABC Waters programme, part of the Kallang River ran through this concrete canal.

Kallang River at Ang Mo Kio-Bishan Park, Singapore.

1   Thomas Schröpfer, *Dense+Green Cities: Architecture as Urban Ecosystem* (Basel, Switzerland: Birkhäuser, 2020).
2   Peter Rowe and Limin Hee, *A City in Blue and Green: The Singapore Story* (Singapore: Springer Verlag, 2019).

LIVING TOGETHER: THE BENEFITS OF HIGH DENSITY VS. THE CURSE OF OVERCROWDING

MOHAMMAD ALASAD

The built environment, with its buildings and spaces, is a resource. As with any resource, its value is determined by supply and demand. The demand for buildings and spaces in the built environment usually supersedes their supply in large human settlements, at least over extended periods of time. As a result, inhabitants try to make the most of them, which translates into high levels of population densities.

High density can, of course, be good considering that we greatly benefit from proximity. As more of us occupy a given area, more options relating to the quantity and variety of services in that area become available. This is an example of economies of scale at work. We therefore do need to live together, but we also need to ensure that our buildings and open spaces can easily accommodate the spatial limitations that often accompany our living together.

High densities, however, can also result in overcrowding. When two siblings share a bedroom in their family's apartment or house, it is considered a healthy living condition that fosters a closer relationship between them. When ten people have to live in a single room, as is common in slum areas across the Global South, the result is miserable and degrading living conditions.

It is in the case of shelter—amongst our most basic of needs—that the issue of density is of uttermost significance. Achieving density while avoiding overcrowding, however, also applies to the structures in which we study, work, shop, receive healthcare, etc., as well as to the open spaces in our human settlements and to conduits of mobility, primarily streets and sidewalks.

An important question for which we do not yet have adequate answers is: where does healthy density give way to the miseries of overcrowding? We can identify conditions of healthy density and suffocating overcrowding, but we still are not able to appropriately define the gray zone in between where one condition begins to give in to the other.

One issue that has struck me about the overly prevalent danger of healthy densities giving way to overcrowding is that both the poorest cities in the world and the richest are susceptible to it. We are too well aware of the bidonvilles, favelas, gecekondus, and kampungs taking over the cities of the Global South, but we also should keep in mind that such affluent cities as Hong Kong, London, New York, Paris, or Vancouver—among many others—

have become highly unaffordable. The vast majority of people in those cities, except for the very rich, are increasingly forced to live in (and very often share) cramped living quarters.

Architectural and urban design, of course, can contribute to enhancing the benefits of high density and limiting the damages of overcrowding, but their effectiveness is very limited when compared to public policies that address issues such as equity, environmental protection, and good governance.

Human beings are highly resilient and resourceful, and we usually show a remarkable ability to adapt to very difficult living conditions, including those connected to overcrowding. Still, far too many people are continuously finding themselves having to test the limits of this resilience and resourcefulness in the face of adversity. The more we can change that condition, the better.

Mohammad al-Asad is an architect and urbanist, as well as an architectural and urban historian. He is the Founding Director of the Center for the Study of the Built Environment in Amman (CSBE; www .csbe.org), an independent, private, non-profit think/ do tank that was established in 1999.

Dinu Lazar, Fez, Morocco, general view.

Chromatograph, Hong Kong, general view.

SMALL IS BEAUTIFUL: BEYOND THE MEGACITY'

The rapid pace of urbanization over the past three decades has produced megacities of staggering size and complexity. Most are located in the developing world or the Global South: in China alone, there are five cities with populations over ten million. Architects are fascinated by the megacity phenomenon and have produced vast quantities of research and documentation on the subject. Dense urban development, mass transit, and preserving adjacent open space are inherently green strategies, but megacities have also been marked by segregation and economic inequality, environmental degradation, overburdened infrastructure, and long commute times as they sprawl at the edges. In reality, the discipline of architecture has been powerless to offer practical proposals in the face of the complex economic, social, and political forces shaping the megacity. Two questions are worth asking: Should architects persist in the naïve belief that they could have a meaningful impact on the megacity? And is the proliferation of megacities actually a viable solution to the problems of global urbanism?

In any given country, smaller cities will always vastly outnumber very large cities. This phenomenon, known as Zipf's law, was first noted by Felix Auerbach in 1913.[2] In the United States, for example, the Office of Management and Budget has defined 536 micropolitan statistical areas: urban aggregations with a core population between ten and fifty thousand, and a positive integration of core and surrounding area. Hence a counter-proposition: the *microcity* as both a viable model for living together, and a productive locus for urban research and design. At a time when small size and agility have become watchwords for innovation, it seems relevant for our discipline to rethink its preoccupation with bigness.

Rather than a definitive proposition, this series of open-ended questions might provoke research and creative design work. Beyond scale, what are the essential characteristics that define a city? Are density, diversity, economic and personal mobility, and social cohesion exclusively the properties of large cities? What specific forms of physical organization foster these positive urban traits? What is the specific agency of architecture to shape urban institutions and patterns of living? What *is* the smallest viable urban unit? How can we refigure the relationship between the city and nature? Could a web of smaller cities offer the social, cultural and environmental benefits of urbanism with a lighter ecological footprint?

In place of hyper-developed city centers and radiating sprawl, *microcities* propose a distributed model of density that recognizes the complex interdependency of city and region. And while it is clear that the proliferation of digital technologies has blurred conventional relationships between city and countryside, technology alone is not the answer. Only through creative imagination and the accumulated knowledge of the discipline will it be possible to imagine a dynamic network of microcities as a viable response to the social, economic, and environmental challenges of global urbanism today.

Stan Allen is an architect working in New York and George Dutton '27 Professor of Architecture at Princeton University. His most recent publication is: *Situated Objects: Building and Projects by Stan Allen* (Park Books, 2020).

1   My title refers to E. F. Schumacher's 1973 collection of essays *Small is Beautiful: A Study of Economics as if People Mattered*, which in part triggered these speculations.

2   Felix Auerbach, "Das Gesetz der Bevölkerungskonzentration" (The Law of Population Concentration), *Petermanns Geographische Mitteilungen* 59 (1913): 73–76. First formulated in the 1940s by American linguist George Kingsley Zipf, the law states that the frequency of any word is inversely proportional to its rank among all other words: the most frequent word will occur approximately twice as often as the second most frequent word, three times as often as the third most frequent word, etc. Many researchers and commentators have noted the close fit to city population. See for example Edward L. Glaeser, "A Tale of Many Cities," *Economix* (blog), *New York Times*, April 20, 2010, https://economix.blogs.nytimes.com/2010/04/20/a-tale-of-many-cities/.

Karl Ludwig Hilberseimer,
The City in the Landscape, 1944.

STAN ALLEN

EXISTENZMINIMUM

FILE COPY 1651

What sort of homes do British workers want?
How many rooms? What rents? and 1001
other major questions are tackled in this
ADVERTISING SERVICE GUILD'S REPORT ON

People's Homes

CONDUCTED BY MASS-OBSERVATION

This, the fourth national survey spon-
sored by the Advertising Service Guild,
deals with the problems which perplex
all those who have tried (and are trying)
to consider what housing policy should
be followed after the war. It is the most
exhaustive enquiry ever made into these
problems and provides data likely to
prove invaluable to architects, sociologists,
politicians, civil servants and thousands
of other specialists and technicians.

Plans and Projects
Own or Rent?
Gardens
Town v Country
Flats v Houses
Lighting and Heating
Hygiene
Travel and Shopping

PRICE TEN SHILLINGS

HADAS A. SIEBER

Since the turn of the last century, the sense of social crisis has diverted architectural attention toward the fundamentals of shelter. From the case for the democratic lessons of the bourgeois interior made by Hermann Muthesius in *The English House* (1904), to the search for the minimal components of dwelling on display at the *Weissenhofseidlung* (1927), the pursuit of basic architectural requirements for a meaningful existence prevailed. Variation in the choice of precedent, or details of the final proposal, laid bare the disparate politics at play in a profession redefining itself as modern. Housing could be heralded as an emancipatory project, or as Le Corbusier outlined in the final chapter of *Vers une architecture* (1923), it could be deployed to keep the masses in check. The values that governed the collective shaped the house.

Domestic ambitions were heightened again in the decades following World War II, but with a significant conceptual twist. As demonstrated in the iconic "Urban Reidentification" *grille* (1953) presented at CIAM 9 by Peter and Alison Smithson, the contours of the house—rather than its function—generated urban configurations. These forms were based in patterns of social engagement that were to be extrapolated from the interactions of the family at increasingly greater scales. If the organization of society at large was to be generated by the criteria of an acceptable social unit, the basic requirements that now shaped the collective were of individual fulfillment. By the mid-sixties, ideas of what constituted a family changed and so did the form of the shell. Personal needs were boldly featured in the domestic visions of the neo-avant-garde, as the quintessential space of daily life became an aspirational model to explore an architecture ever more responsive to the input of desire.

Interest in neo-avant-garde objectives has been revived as once imagined technologies have come to fruition, but who are the imagined inhabitants of our current idealized conception of the home? From the masses to the family and the individual, the answer of the profession to this query at any given time reveals much about the ability of an architectural ideology to face upheaval in the public domain. Nowhere, for example, is the segregation of the American city more concrete than in its approach to housing, which continues to divide society by class and color. When people, whether in their socially-sanctioned

Hadas A. Steiner is an Associate Professor at the University at Buffalo, SUNY. She is at work on a manuscript, *The Accidental Visitant*, which studies the impact of ornithology on the conceptualization of the built environment as an ecosystem.

familial configurations or as individuals, are validated predominantly through their status as legal entities, the social indicators reified by architecture must be scrutinized. Living collectively requires more attention to what is at stake in the emphasis of basic needs, whether individual or communal. To critically address what has been assumed as elemental can helps us in the effort to realize the freedoms of society that are still only imagined to be.

Humphrey Spender, *Stepney Washer Women*, 1934.

Mass-Observation, Cover for *An Enquiry Into People's Homes: A Report Prepared by Mass-Observation for the Advertising Service Guild, the Fourth of the "Change" Wartime Surveys*. London: John Murray, 1943.

HADAS A. STEINER

ARCHITECTURE IS NOT NECESSARILY FUNCTIONALIST

BIOSPHERE
THE GLOBAL INFRASTRUCTURE

YONA FRIEDMAN

Architecture and design in the twentieth century were functionalist, best defined by Frank Lloyd Wright: "form follows function."

Strangely enough, sciences like biology, sociology, etc., don't follow that principle. Function can follow any form.

Functionalism in architecture meant that floor plans, sections, etc., had to be organized following a conventional scheme, assumed to be optimal to the user's behavior pattern. The Bauhaus attitude was a beacon for functionalism.

When I started in the late 1950s with my project, Mobile Architecture, I contested the existence of average optimal schemes. "Optimal," in my mind was a reference that needed to be personalized, from case to case, and from year to year.

Architecture has to be changeable; walls, floors, openings should be as "moveable" as chairs and tables. My proposal, Ville Spatiale, presented technical solutions for mobility: components of moveable architecture that can be inserted into a space-frame "infrastructure," itself raised on distant staircase-pillars, in order to minimize foundations (which are, by their nature, fixed).

I proposed that the disposition of premises should be decided by the actual inhabitant, using for this task a "trial and error" process that can be ultimately improvised.

The Villa Spatiale is not "functional" in the sense of mainstream architecture.

At the beginning of the twenty-first century I tried to get rid of the material "infrastructure," considering that new technology and ecological sensibility permitted an immaterial "cloud infrastructure." I proposed what I call the Meuble Plus concept: small cabin-like volumes, containing particular furniture plus the space necessary for its use (that is of "meuble plus"). Thus, the living premises—the house—would become an assembly of such cabins that could be pushed around, as is done with ordinary furniture. Function would follow the potentially irrational preference of the inhabitant.

Excerpt from "Biosphere: The Global Infrastructure" (2017) Courtesy of the Fonds de Dotation Denise et Yona Friedman.

Yona Friedman (1923–2020) was a Hungarian-born French architect. Starting in 1958 with his manifesto "L' Architecture Mobile," he has since been the subject of numerous retrospectives, and his drawings and models are part of the permanent collections at MoMA in New York, the Pompidou Center in Paris, the Victoria and Albert Museum in London, the Getty Institute in Los Angeles, and the French National collections.

YONA FRIEDMAN

Yona Friedman, *Sketch*, 2016.

201

RUPALI GUPTE

SMUDGED
SPACES

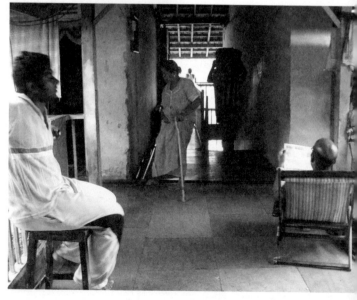

The Chawl House

Little Sharan rides his tricycle through the porous house of Janki and her ailing husband, across the bridge, over a courtyard, between the two wings of the Poonawala Chawl—a working class building in Mumbai. On the bridge, Dominique sits in a chair reading a newspaper, oblivious to Shanta and Durga, who are fighting over the use of the common toilets. Reshma calls out to her daughter playing with her friends on a large trunk on the mid-landing of the staircase. No one remembers who put the trunk there. It has become collective property, like the multitude of other orphaned furniture items around. The corridor widens into a balcony, where Rahima sits with her crutches watching the street. In Janki's house, the shutter of the kitchen cabinet, like a Duchampian door, toggles between its day and night positions to secure the house at night. In the absence of monetized social security, visitors who keep tabs on the old couple fill the gap. Poonawala Chawl acts like one big house.

The Forest House

A Warli painting on a wall in Jayshree's house shows an imagined home: a pentagon with a pitched roof hut inscribed inside, it is a place where elements of nature—the sun, the moon, a tortoise, birds—and mundane household objects like a comb, a ladder, etc., comingle. Outside the house are a set of stylized human stick figures intermingling with animals and vegetation and engaged in a festive dance. The house deity resides in the attic. The forest house is made with ephemeral materials—mud and dung pasted over a mesh of reed obtained from the forest. The house is renewed every two years, contributing to the rhythm of life of the inhabitants. The villagers worship two gods: the green god, *hirwa dev*, and the tiger God, *wagh dev*. This is an impermanent house, which is continuous with the landscape.

The Street House

Naseem's house on Lamington road, a very busy market street, becomes a warehouse at night. It forms the first layer of a dense palimpsest of inhabitations. The second layer is comprised of shops, which sell computer peripherals, all connected by an internal intercom system. The third layer is made of "one-foot" shops embedded in the walls of the building. They pay rent to the

RUPALI GUPTE

shop behind. The fourth layer is the series of vendors on the pavement. At night their shops are tethered to a post or a manhole, others are watched over by the homeless who sleep on the pavement or kept in homes such as Naseem's for a small fee. The map shows a single line between the street and the building in which Naseem lives. However, on the ground, this line corrodes, blurs, and thickens to create a dense network of relationships.

The chawl, forest, and street house have evolved historically out of lived relationships. These spaces blur boundaries between the public and private, the inside and outside, the dark and lit, the propertied and claimed, and the built and unbuilt, to create a democratic space that offers clues for how we could live in a future that is cellular, where resources are limited and the population is ageing. "Democratic" here does not mean without contradictions. Attempts to erase contradictions have produced spaces with high polarities and inequities. Instead we look for clues in spaces that settle slowly, with all their contradictions, but where lived relations are slowly built through negotiations.

Rupali Gupte is an architect, urbanist, and artist based in Mumbai. She is a Professor at the School of Environment and Architecture (SEA) and a partner at BardStudio. Her work often crosses disciplinary boundaries and takes different forms— writings, drawings, mixed-media works, story-telling, teaching, conversations, walks, spatial interventions, and curation.

Chawl House, Poonawala Chawl, Mumbai.

SHARING
IS
CARING

January 25, 2020.

To live more generously may imply a more radical and unhindered arrangement between our personal belongings and the common good. The production of every object we own—and every immaterial asset we take advantage of—involves a broader societal effort and the transformation of resources that amply exceed their market cost. In this sense, the idea of individual property reveals itself as unsustainable, and inconsistent with the possibility of an equal society. Materials, technologies, computing power, even the embedded time of their production and the space they occupy when not in use, are assets borrowed from the environment. They're all limited resources that cannot be owned on a private basis; we should move away from a concept of exclusive, personal use, and think instead of how to recirculate their universal value.

The sharing economy—which has been thriving on thousands of platforms for over a decade—can help us to collectively and securely benefit from our material world. One of its positive aspects is certainly the fact that people are enabled to access things and services they might not otherwise be able to afford. Yet, would it be possible to extend its reach in order to overcome its current, limited influence on our lives? The spaces we inhabit and the objects we own remain unused for many hours a day while we spend time away from them. What if carpooling were the only reasonable mode of "owning" a car? What if we could share our domestic spaces in a more flexible and generous way than the profit-driven manipulation of real estate capital operated by AirBnB?

A film by Kim Ki-duk speculates about this possibility. One of the protagonists of *3-Iron* breaks into apartments while their owners are away, taking care of their belongings and doing ordinary maintenance. What prevents us from feeling at home—even if only for a few hours—in different places? And what keeps us tied to the exclusivity of our own spaces, so that we feel violated when they are used by others?

In an article for the *New York Times*, Lindsay T. Graham, a space researcher and social psychologist at the Center for Built Environment at the University of California, Berkeley states: "If we've taken the time and effort to put our personalities into our environments and to feel connected with them and express ourselves through them, inviting others in puts us in a vulnerable position.

It may sound cheesy, but you're handing a piece of yourself over to a stranger who might not respect it. You're renting out part of your identity."[1]

Some people are incapable of detaching themselves from the belongings they own and share only with the ones who are dear to them. After a bad experience while renting out his apartment, the protagonist of *Selling Dreams*, a film directed by Ila Bêka and Louise Lemoine, decides to inhabit hotel rooms and make a living by selling the short-term dream of his beautiful flats to strangers. If private space were more accessible, the film suggests, people of all origins would have access to houses whose owners' presence could be gleaned through their interiors, their furniture, appliances, books, objects, and memories of all sorts. This scenario might be an ideal very difficult to reach when we start to consider all the implications.

The sharing economy is a first step toward realizing that each object has an intrinsic value that belongs to the society at large: this value cannot be bought by the transaction of a personal purchase because objects use technologies and resources to be produced, that we can only borrow from the common good *par excellence*—the environment.

Studio Folder is a Milan-based interdisciplinary research and design agency founded by Marco Ferrari and Elisa Pasqual. The studio's work spans between the cultural and the commercial domains and self-initiated projects, whilst working through a diverse range of outcomes—from data visualization, both for physical and online spaces to the design of exhibitions, printed media, editorial products, art direction, and visual identity consultancy.

We own space due to social super-structures inherited throughout history—but the feeling we have is that space property is an outdated concept at best, that perpetrates social exclusion, inequalities, and discriminations.

To live more generously together we imagine an utopia where spaces are considered to be common goods accessible by everyone, and where the saying "sharing is caring" is applied not only to specific tangible objects but also to more personal and intimate spheres such as our homes.

1   Diane Stopyra, "When You Give Your House Keys to a Stranger," *New York Times*, August 16, 2019, https://www.nytimes.com/2019/08/16/realestate/when-you-give-your-house-keys-to-a-stranger.html.

LILAC:
A BOLD EXPERIMENT
IN LOW-IMPACT
COMMUNAL LIVING

"How will we live together?" It is a question that neither governments nor private developers have been able to answer convincingly in the UK for years. Homelessness has doubled since 2010, one in three millennials will never be able to afford their own home, and people of all ages now report feeling more lonely and isolated than ever before.

But one radical answer can be found in an unlikely location on the edge of suburban Leeds in the north of England. Among the redbrick Victorian terraced streets of Bramley, set back from the street on a raised brick plinth, a cluster of little wooden buildings stands in a lush communal garden, with an area of productive allotments beyond. This is LILAC, the Low Impact Living Affordable Community, a development of twenty homes that represents a revolutionary model of low-carbon collective living, which will remain affordable to local people in perpetuity.

Completed in 2013, it is the UK's first Mutual Home Ownership Society (MHOS), a radical form of tenure that allows people of all backgrounds and incomes to have a stake in the community. Developers and politicians love to talk of creating "mixed communities," but this truly is one: the residents range from single people in their twenties to retired couples in their seventies, spanning from university lecturers to professional storytellers, bouncers, and more.

A common house, including a collective laundry room, workshop, and toolshed, means that individual homes are not cluttered with the usual paraphernalia of washing machines, vacuum cleaners, and lawn mowers, as all of these things are shared, while a large dining room allows for the occasional cooking and eating together. Community bonds were also forged during the construction process: the buildings' structure comprises a prefabricated system of timber frames, which the residents helped to packed with straw bales, before they were sprayed with lime render. But the real innovation is in the form of tenure, setting this apart from other forms of cooperative living.

"People can sometimes get trapped living in co-ops, because they can't afford to leave," says Tash Gordon, a doctor and founding member of the LILAC group. "This way, everyone has equity in the project, so you can realize your stake if you decide to move on."

A Mutual Home Ownership Society is a way of owning a stake in the housing market, designed to bring property ownership back within reach of households on modest incomes in areas where they are priced out. All residents pay 35% of their net income into a trust and receive a corresponding number of equity shares in the project, meaning those on salaries of £15,000 can still get a rung on the housing ladder. After deductions for costs like maintenance and insurance, these payments pay the mortgage, and it is the society and not the individuals that obtains the mortgage, so borrowing is cheaper—in this case, it takes the form of a loan from the Triodos ethical bank.

So far, LILAC represents a tiny experiment, but it is one that deserves to be repeated.

Oliver Wainwright is the architecture and design critic of the *Guardian*. He trained as an architect and has worked for OMA, Muf, and the Architecture and Urbanism Unit of the Greater London Authority. He is a regular visiting critic and lecturer at a number of architecture schools; his first book, *Inside North Korea*, was published by Taschen in 2018.

LILAC: Low Impact Living Affordable Community.

HOW WE SPENT OUR VACATIONS TOGETHER: SOCIAL HOUSING FOR HOLIDAYS IN FRANCE IN THE 1960S AND 1970S

During the 1960s and 1970s, holiday villages for the working classes were built in France in coastal and rural areas. At the beginning of the 1960s, like today, hotels were often too expensive and not very suitable for family life for the underprivileged social classes. So too was camping, which required equipment that had to be bought and stored. To provide holiday resorts to low-income social classes, holiday villages were built and managed by numerous private and public actors.[1] Sixty years later, some of these residences have been sold and transformed to meet the needs of wealthier populations, while others, due to lack of investment and maintenance, are facing destruction.

Sponsors of Social Housing for Holidays

The Beg-Meil Holiday Village, designed by architect Henri Mouette in collaboration with sculptors Pierre and Véra Szekely in 1971–1972, is the most original example of these residences and testifies to both progressive and spiritual concerns.[2] It offers spaces for collective reflection and discussion and provides shelter for the temporary community that constitutes the village, while offering several types of comfortable and quality places to stay.

The village was constructed by Renouveau Vacances, a nonprofit association founded by Pierre and Janine Lainé, a couple of Catholic activists, together with a group of families in 1954. The aim was to promote holidays for families with modest income.[3] In 1971, in parallel with Beg-Meil, the association launched the ski resort, Les Karellis, with Guy Rey-Millet and the Atelier d'Architecture en Montagne, known for the creation of the resort Les Arcs with Charlotte Perriand. Renouveau Vacances built seventeen mountain and seafront residences in the 1950s and '70s, with a team of volunteers and seventy-five permanent staff, and prices adapted to its residents' resources.

Team X member Georges Candilis also built many holiday homes on the Mediterranean coast. According to him, the 1933 Athens Charter did not take into account the notion of leisure.[4] For the development of Port Leucate (1962–1976), which includes 3,500 housing units, he adapted, among other models, the principle of the patio house on a serial composition.

The Creation of an Original Architectural Landscape

The Beg-Meil Holiday Village testifies both to the rejection of the modern mat and to the principle of the series. Voluntarily at once

212

strange and singular, it is close to the architecture proposed by Jean Balladur at La Grande Motte. In search of a renewal of the architectural vocabulary, opposed to the aesthetics of the CIAMs, and driven by the desire to create a site on a marsh landscape, Beg-Meil's architecture is based on the idea of implementing a living environment that promotes new forms of sociability between holidaymakers—a concern inseparable from a spiritual quest, which led him to use strange, sculptural, and lyrical architectural forms.

Even if Henri Mouette was well acquainted with the modern canonical forms of holiday residence architecture and had collaborated on the Courchevel ski resort project within the Atelier d'Architecture en Montagne, he chose the expressive character of sculptural forms for the collective spaces of this village in Brittany. In order to promote encounters between holidaymakers, he designed unusual and inspiring spaces. The avowed ambition was to incite people to imagine a new way of life that favors collective behavior and values instead of individualism.

Many villages built for popular tourism today illustrate the abandonment of the social project that gave birth to them. Thanks to its original architecture, Beig-Meil has remained faithful to the original ideal of its designers. It gives shape to a form of "living together" that appears as necessary today as it was in the past.

Virginie Picon-Lefebvre is an architect and an urbanist. She holds a PhD in Art history from Université de la Sorbonne, and is a professor at the École d'Architecture Paris-Belleville. She taught at the École d'Architecture de Paris Versailles and Paris-Malaquais and was a lecturer at the GSD, Harvard University. She did research about modernist projects in Paris. Her most recent book is about the architecture of tourism.

Mouette Architects, Beg Meil Holiday Village at the end of construction, France.

Mouette Architects, Beg Meil Holiday Village, Dining Room.

George Candilis, Vacation Village in Port Leucate, France, Welcome Desk.

1   See Virginie Picon-Lefebvre, *La Fabrique du bonheur* (Marseille: Éditions Parenthèses, 2019), 154–170.

2   Daniell Le Couédic, "Le Village Renouveau de Beg-Meil: une pastorale hédoniste," in *Mémoires de la Société d'histoire et d'archéologie de Bretagne* 97 (2019): 251–278.

3   Philippe Rousselot, "Chronique de l'association Renouveau: une histoire emblématique du tourisme associative," *Cahiers Espaces*, no. 94 (August 2007): 57–66.

4   Georges Candilis, *Recherches sur l'architecture des loisirs* (Paris: Eyrolles, 1973), 140.

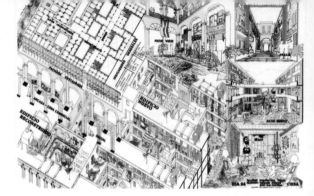

THE PARALLEL UTOPIA: THE NEW HUMAN AND ITS URBAN DREAMS IN CUBA

IVÁN DE LA NUEZ

An unheard-of project took place in Cuba during the 1980s. A Western-like urbanism, in the absence both of market relations and public developers, was designed. It held the proposition for a collective utopia that was, paradoxically, ignored by the socialist State, and activated a movement that began as a critique of the architecture of the time, yet today hangs like the sword of Damocles over the conspicuous constructions State capitalism enables. This history feels especially prescient today, as the very plausible "Shanghaization" of Havana seems to loom around the corner, accompanied by its corresponding drive toward totemic buildings (largely, hotels), lacking any consideration whatsoever for the spaces where they stand.

In order to think formally about living together, it may be worthwhile to recover the urban strategies conceived by the generation of architects who were born with the Cuban Revolution and projected their dreams throughout the eighties.

Years before, Che Guevara had advanced the definition of the New Human as a subject uncontaminated by capitalism and prepared to grow in a classless society. By the 1980s, a parallel utopia was thus not so much about particular buildings as about urban dreams. It was about understanding the city as a conversation between building and imagining, heritage and futurism, urbanism and popular invention, architecture and urban scale. As a consequence, most projects radically abandoned the common stereotypes of Cuban cities—and in particular of Havana—to explore the possibilities of an *architettura povera* which might, however, allow Cuban society to advance towards the future. While this utopia originated in the field of architecture, its final goal was never to operate within the discipline's limits. Its proposals could be read as essays, drafts of a city to come that favored cultural plurality over the State's single, ideological vision.

This movement recognized, for instance, the contributions made toward the recovery and conservation of Havana, which was declared a World Heritage Site in 1982, but it also attributed a crucial role to the subaltern city, thus repudiating the vision of a palace-like reconstruction of Havana which replicated, once and again, the old colonial power.

When dreaming their cities, no urban projects were unknown to these architects: neither Robert Venturi's learning from everything, nor Aldo Rossi's travels across history; neither Philip Johnson's potential, high-tech landing in Havana's Malecón, nor Denise Scott Brown's "socially responsible architecture."

All these ideas occured without forgetting the masters who tried to build other utopias from 1959 on: Ricardo Porro, Vittorio Garatti, Roberto Gottardi, Walter Betancourt, and Gilberto Séguì-Diviño. This urbanism knew no prejudices: it was equally capable of proposing a Congódromo (honoring percussionist Chano Pozo), as it was a celebration of the two-hundredth anniversary of French Revolution, in both cases using the visual language of Carnival.

When Eastern European communism fell, the protagonists of this parallel utopia could not see themselves as the citizens of the post-industrial world Lyotard described. Nor could they identify with the "big project of Reason" Habermas proposed. But they could understand that part of the Big Bang that exploded in Berlin would resonate on the island, and that its waves would affect them forever.

The time of this parallel utopia began with the Mariel exodus in 1980 and concluded in 1993, the year the dollar became legal currency on the island and the crises of the *balseros* (rafters) and the *Maleconazo* started appearing in the horizon. This utopian architecture unfolded between these two moments of Cuban history. It was a critical architecture which, paradoxically, could only exist within a socialist system. A collective utopia obsessed with turning architecture into city and city into citizenship.

This text evokes The Parallel Utopia, *an exhibition curated by Iván de la Nuez in collaboration with Atelier Morales, La Virreina-Image Center of Barcelona, July–October, 2019, and Museum of Contemporary Art Es Baluard, Palma de Mallorca, April–October, 2020.*

Translated from Spanish by Roi Salgueiro Barrio

Iván de la Nuez is an essayist, critic, and curator. His books include *La balsa perpetua* (The Perpetual Raft), *El mapa de sal Fantasía Roja* (The Red Fantasy Salt Map), *El comunista manifiesto* (The Manifest Communist), *Teoría de la retaguardia* (Theory of the Rearguard), and *Cubantropía*. He has curated numerous exhibitions, the most recent of which, *The Parallel Utopia: Dream Cities in Cuba, 1980–1993*, inspires his text for this book.

Rosendo Mesías and Juan Luis Morales, Urban and architectural renewal project, *Architecture at the Service of Users*, Havana, Cuba, 1983. Award Emilio Pérez Piñero from the Consejo Superior de Colegios de Arquitectura of Spain (1984). International Competition of Architecture Students. International Union of Architects, Paris (1984).

Teresa Ayuso and Juan Luis Morales, *La Ciudad Invisible (Invisible City)*, Italo Calvino, IV Havana Biennale, Cuba, 1991.

LIVING TOGETHER AFTER MASS VIOLENCE

DELIA DUONG BA WENDEL

DELIA DUONG BA WENDEL

After the 1994 genocide, the Rwandan government employed architecture and urban planning to build peace. Authorities required all residents to move from scattered homesteads into newly constructed villages. Identical houses were built in equally spaced, gridded plots. Villagization brought diverse residents together after the chaos of mass violence—including former perpetrators, genocide survivors, and returnees from long-term exile. However, the program's effects have not all been positive. In many cases, villagization has restricted civil liberties, disrupted social cohesion, and negatively affected livelihoods. The new villages endeavor to suspend the afterlives of the genocide while imagining and enacting a new and different reality.

In 2013, I asked the same question of every rural resident in Rwanda that I met: "If you were to visit another village, how would you know if peace was there?"[1] I was asking individuals if peace was more than an ideal. I was inquiring into the everyday conditions and challenges for peace in the intervening twenty years.

Residents typically claim that new villages structure peace. They draw from quotidian examples, like sharing water and land, tending kitchen fires for neighbors, and watching each other's children. Villagization has had real impacts on forms of sociality. In the two decades since the genocide, fear, distrust, and the grief of loss have had to be suspended or overcome for these everyday interactions to take place. Residents recount how neighborliness, daily repetition, and living proximity have helped to assuage such feelings. These social practices and built environments co-constitute a lived peace, even if it is not completely intact or consistently embraced.

However, residents who do not fully agree with this view are skeptical of the appearance of peace and order that the new villages represent. Many are also very poor and socially stigmatized as a result of ethnic identity, familial relationships to genocide perpetrators, or convictions for genocide crimes. For these residents, villages are not more secure. Relocating requires land exchanges that makes earning a living more precarious and brings residents closer to neighbors that regard them with suspicion. Villages reproduce existing tensions and create a more intense environment for reconciliation. In these cases, peace maps unevenly onto class inequality and social identity.

Rwanda's villagization experiment conceives of peace as an imagined community—one that exists partly as an ideal and partly in the world. The government's version of this imagined community suggests that peace is a matter of development: of housing and rural urbanization. Evoking parallels to early twentieth-century new towns, Rwanda's villagization program uses modernist aesthetics and planning to represent Rwandan society as progressive, unified, and reconciled. Not merely concerned with nation building, villagization is as much a product of "liberal peace" orthodoxy—an international paradigm that insists that economic development produces stability and peace. Yet, there is violence in this form of peacebuilding. Liberal peace strategies tend to privilege elite and foreign political and economic interests. Many of Rwanda's new villages spatially stratify citizens and outcasts, suppress difference, and regulate political life. As a result, villagization poorly addresses local challenges to living together after mass violence.

In Rwanda, as elsewhere, the imperative of peace is not in itself sufficient to articulating or resolving the dilemmas that arise in "the space of concrete problems, dangers, and hopes."[2] The key is to recognize that peace is a *process* of realizing an imagined community. It is not to take peacebuilding initiatives as self-evident, but rather to be more attentive to the ruptures and conflicts that those architecture and planning projects produce.

Delia Duong Ba Wendel explores the politics of memory and geographies of conflict in East Africa and the United States. She is an Assistant Professor of Urban Studies at the Massachusetts Institute of Technology.

Pre-1994 typical habitat pattern, with homes loosely oriented to a dirt access road

Post-1994 village settlements, with houses uniformly spaced in grid plans.

1 For 21 months during 2011–2013, I conducted a study of peacebuilding in Rwanda employing a combination of ethnographic, spatial, survey, oral history, and archival research. I asked this question of 614 people in 36 villages. Fieldwork was generously supported by the Social Science Research Council's International Dissertation Research Fellowship, the Harvard Sheldon Traveling Fellowship, the Harvard Weatherhead Center for International Affairs, and the Harvard Humanitarian Institute. Writing was supported by the Harvard Safra Center for Ethics and a Mellon/American Council for Learned Societies Dissertation Completion Fellowship.

2 Paul Rabinow, "Midst Anthropology's Problems," *Cultural Anthropology* 17, no. 2 (May 2002): 145.

SUSTAINED FLIGHT: KISHI KOTA'S ATOMIC ARCHITECTURE

Fukushima, Japan. 2013.

Kishi Kota's *Garecki Heart Mother* (2014) combines nomadism, wreckage (*garecki*), and photography. Its setting is the earthquake, tsunami, and nuclear meltdown in Fukushima that struck Japan on March 11, 2011. Since that record clobbering disaster, pro-nuclear Japan has poached the conceit of "recycling" to rebrand the removal of radioactive topsoil and promote nuclear power. But tainted soil cannot be incinerated. By 2013, paddy fields in Fukushima prefecture were choking under bags of toxic material. It was then that Kishi engineered a reverse heist, reclaiming this purloined conceit.

From March to September 2013, Kishi trawled Fukushima's coastline for wreckage that he refashioned into architecture, arks, and visitants. Each endeavor produced a photograph titled by date and place. A single day could inspire numerous configurations including buoys, floorboards, tarps, and children's car seats.

The dense postcard boxset of Kishi's original printing became a C-shaped exhibit at Photographers Gallery in Tokyo. One hundred small photos, juxtaposed on a ledge, charted passage across hostile territory. At stake was the fate of a tautology. Find, build, shoot, and retreat were less about life lost, more about what Abe Kōbō called "sustained flight."[1]

Garecki Heart Mother was first exhibited in 2016, five years after 3/11. Japan's pro-nuclear power lobbies were gaining in strength, while Fukushima housewives turned barefoot scientists and local activists were testing food, soil, and air for contamination. The moral indignation within the series is also germane to Japan's empathy for all nuclear victims, a kinship formed after the United States tested nuclear weapons on humans in Hiroshima and Nagasaki in 1945.

But Kishi's project is unorthodox in eschewing the glib state cliché of the nuclear, defined in terms of an iron-clad, scientific mystery best left alone by the common populace. Unorthodox also in defecting from standard artspeak about the nuclear, which brims with post-apocalyptic test sites, soundtracks of suspenseful static, and fatalism about the age of the Anthropocene. Decades of hard-won nuclear intelligence by field activists and displaced communities tell a different story.

An image from Namie-machi shot on April 16, 2013 presents a rare element within the series: a placard with text. "Loading personnel should not exceed six." Directed at the sculpture behind, the injunction feels odd. The sculpture is made of boat debris reassembled to resemble a lifeguard perch. The palette—cerulean blue, diamine green, apricot yellow, light glaucous blue—could be straight out of Wada Sanzō's elegant Shōwa period opus, *A Dictionary of Color Combinations* (1931), published when imperial Japan was establishing manuals for everything from the tonality of emotion to the rationale for empire. Axial balance and stability reign, until one notices a bashed-up Toyota Prius, nose-up on the far right. Like the placard, this yellow ruin is anomalous. It breaks with the photographer's protocol to transform wreckage into humor, comfort, and pleasure.

The explanation lies upwind. Namie-machi is a town on the leeward side of the leaking Fukushima Daiichi Nuclear Power Plant. The meltdown of March 2011 forced immediate evacuation. It was a month before searchers were permitted to retrieve tsunami fatalities, and two years before two town quarters were briefly opened up, letting evacuees look for the personal effects of drowned family members. Kishi's image of April 16, 2013 performs a necessary transubstantiation. Mystery to metal. Invisible radiation to visible rust. A destroyed Prius, which no one had been able to dislodge, disproves what Namie-machi's reopening upholds. Residual radiation suffusing the town remains high. Like other areas in Fukushima, it remains a Difficult-to-Return zone, and that much more difficult to leave. Kishi built over twenty configurations in Namie-machi before his eventual retreat.

Prajna Desai is a writer of art history and prose-poetry. Her research and scholarship about visual politics, print culture, and built form develops at the intersection of history, literature, and accounts of nature. She has held teaching positions and fellowships at the University of Southern California (LA), Stern College for Women (NYC), Delfina Foundation (London), The Museum of Modern Art (NYC), and The School of Visual Arts (NYC). She lives in Mumbai.

1   Abe discusses "sustained flight" in three essays from the late 1960s: "The Passport of Heresy" ("Itan no pasupōto," 1968), "The Frontier Within" ("Uchi naru Henkyō," 1968), and "The Frontier Within, Part II" ("Zoku: Uchi naru Henkyō," 1969). The most coherent note appears in the last text through a neologism, nigedashippanashi (逃げ出しっぱなし), which translates literally as "don't stop running:" "The notion that we need to cultivate concerns the state of sustained flight. What does this mean? Whereas settling down somewhere is a basic condition, remaining in a state of sustained flight is a process. We carry within ourselves a prejudice that this process invariably involves settling down somewhere. My point here consists in shedding doubt on this prejudice." See: Abe Kōbō, *The Frontier Within: Essays by Abe Kōbō*, ed. and trans. Richard F. Calichman (New York: Columbia University Press, 2013), 111–148.

Kishi Kota, *008 Namie Fukushima, April 16, 2013, Garecki Heart Mother*, 2014.

SILENT
ASSEMBLY

223

Moments with Saloua Raouda Choucair's sculptures are when I want to possess art. Not so much own it as *hold* it—without compunction, cupping its edges, its oils interacting with mine, and discovering which parts come loose and which stay together. Nearly every sculpture of hers I've encountered is kept under Plexiglas, a doublespeak insult to the assemblies Choucair staged.

Choucair's sculptures reveal their luscious parts, usually made of wood or formed from a cast. Held together by gravity, the parts perform constellations. They're like written words made of signs and letters, that when placed together change shape, and then meaning. Choucair's sculptures are letters made into poems. They are vocabularies and cities. They are as organic as they are mechanic. Letterpresses once mimicked human gestures; then gestures mimicked letterpresses. Whether the letter *q*, or the *aleph*, every character we write or type today is shaped through an exchange between hands and machines. I visualize the ampersand only as forged in steel.

Choucair bristled at what the Western critics ask about "Islamic" art: is it *allowed* to show the human body? In response she proved how the world is assembled and how its particles, even its human bodies, are never irreducible. Like spoken words, or even untranscribed sounds, her work exists only because an entire universe does.

My friend made a book about Choucair's work. Flipping through the pages, she wanted to show me a project she knew I didn't know. The flipping stopped at a kissing, merging family of terra-cottas fired in a kiln. It's a maquette for a bench, she said. Choucair's baked concoction—stripped of context and scale—looked like a denture made for the lower jaw. Its teeth resembled more a forest bed's symbiotic complexity than the machinic columnarity of a human jaw.

If the denture changes into a bench, then one sits along the inner ledge where the tongue rests, when it's not employed to speak or to taste or to lick. When things have settled down, when one has a moment to think about how we got here.

The next page my friend turned to showed a photograph of a place where Choucair's denture got built—its mandible though snapped in two—within a Beirut district destroyed by war before it was devastated by real estate. The developer Solidere built the bench in the late 1990s, just as the last voices opposing the company turned complacent. Artists, designers, and architects were by then complicit in the vanquishing of Beirut.

Today, if only for an interlude, Choucair's ledge offers respite in a Beirut district no longer dead. People are in the streets nearby. Singing songs and sharing chants that abstain from clear demands. No one dares yet say where these demonstrations are heading. There is a kind of silence. An abeyance.

Todd Reisz is an architect and writer. His most recent book is *Showpiece City: How Architecture Made Dubai* (Stanford, 2020).

A plan takes time before taking shape. Silence is a ledge. It's a bed for transforming, for letting shapes make room for each other, for feeling out how we fit together. It's the breath before pulverizing the Plexiglas that swore transparency while it sliced deep the cleft between us.

Saloua Raouda Choucair, *Project for a Bench*, 1969–1971.

BEIRUT, AUGUST 2020: WHAT SHOULD A PLANNER DO?

Every time another disaster strikes the city—and Beirut has sadly seen many disasters—we are solicited as planners to outline *what should be done.* This time was no exception. The massive port blast which rocked the city and its suburbs on August 4, 2020 caused human and material damage equal to a sizable earthquake, and affected more than 250,000 homes. In the days after, it was the usual rush of colleagues, family members, friends, journalists, and students asking me, as a "professional planner:" "How do we rebuild the city? How do we make it more resilient?" Despite the accumulated failure of planners, including locals and foreign experts, to contribute meaningfully in any of the preceding rounds of post-disaster reconstructions, it seems that the *hope* that planning will *guide the recovery process* remains relatively intact. It is further fueled by a handful of senior colleagues, exclusively men, who demand with every round that "the area be placed under study" and "all building activity frozen" until 'we'—read *planners*— "set the rules and guidelines for how to rebuild it." These statements are particularly striking in a city where planners can hardly be credited for organizing anything, whether to respond to crisis or manage everyday urban development.

When asked, "What should we do?" my first instinct is to hide behind the repertoire of grounded research to argue that planning doesn't work. Standing on the shoulders of a tradition identified by planning theorists as "The Dark Side of Planning," it is easy to excel: planning is designed to reproduce power structures and benefit the few.[1] In addition, urban and building regulations are hardly enforced in Lebanon: powerful developers build through exceptions while the urban majorities are either granted temporary permissions or merely tolerated.[2]

But what the crisis really confronts us with, every time, is whether planning *can* be meaningful in these circumstances. What are people looking for when they ask for planning? I posit that the appeal of planning is premised on its promise of championing the common good and demonstrating the possibility of collective coordination for better shared spaces and humane futures. However, in the absence of a custodian of the common good—a role planners have historically associated with democratic and representative political agencies have sometimes occupied— planning becomes a weapon in the hands of warring agents of the state, societies, private interests, and/or other powerful actors who manipulate it at will.[3] The absence of a custodian of the common good in numerous cities should not, however, lead us to revoke the positive potential that planning has by suggesting the possibility for collectivities to come together and imagine, reflect, deliberate, and organize their lives in the spaces they share.

The past decade has been rich with social movements enacting, through their practices, a regenerative vision of collective spaces and their planning. For example, the Occupy Movement in the United States, the Arab Spring in Egypt and Tunisia, or, more recently Lebanon's uprising, have provided powerful models of the progressive potential of the profession of city planning. The audacious occupation of abandoned theaters, parking lots, city streets, and public squares in numerous cities amounts to a disruptive repertoire of action, one that defies the dominant logic of capital. In addition, the activities introduced into public urban spaces such as soup kitchens, free psychiatric clinics, public debates, and artistic performances, among others, inject lasting possibilities that should provide unique inspiration for planners and architects invested in the progressive potential of our professions. They require us to invent the institutional frameworks that can shift these temporary tactics into long-term, sustainable strategies of city-making. This same imperative animates many Lebanese planners in the current post-disaster context of Beirut, where numerous nonprofit organizations, solidarity movements, and private actors are enacting the imaginary of a planning process that could orient the future development of the city towards the collective interest.

In an essay reflecting on the role of the critic, Bruno Latour has argued for extending the role of criticism beyond pointing out limitations.[4] He challenges critics to offer "the participants arenas in which to gather."[5] It is the potential of planning to offer these arenas, to provide individuals—through deliberations over the present and future of the places they occupy collectively—the possibility of imagining their lives together, within the spaces they share, that I believe is precious and worthy of recovering. Rather than assuming the possibility of a custodian of the planning process in preexisting collectivities, as is usually done through formal planning processes, the activist practices of the past decades have offered pathways and models for how collaborative practices can be built in space. There is a lot that planners can

Mona Fawaz is Professor in Urban Studies and Planning at the American University of Beirut where she has co-founded the Beirut Urban Lab, a regional research center invested in working towards more inclusive, just, and viable cities. Mona is involved in her city, Beirut, by publishing and speaking in numerous local venues where advocates for protecting the urban commons, improving livability, adopting inclusive planning standards come together.

learn from these practices to foster the making of shared platforms on which individuals from otherwise fractured positions can assemble.

1   Oren Yiftachel, "Social Control, Urban Planning and Ethno-class Relations: Mizhrahi Jews in Israel's 'Development Towns'," *International Journal of Urban and Regional Research* 24, no. 2 (June 2020): 418-438.

2   See Mona Fawaz, "Exceptions and the Actually Existing Practice of Planning: Beirut (Lebanon) as Case Study," *Urban Studies* 54, no. 8 (June 2017): 1938–1955.

3   See Hiba Bou Akar, *For the War Yet to Come: Planning Beirut's Frontiers* (Stanford, CA: Stanford University Press, 2018).

4   See Bruno Latour, "Why Has Critique Run Out of Steam? From Matters of Fact to Matters of Concern," *Critical Inquiry* 30, no. 2 (Winter 2004): 225–245.

5   Latour, 246.

MONA FAWAZ

from top left clockwise: View over Armenia Street after the Beirut Port explosion on August 4, 2020.

Removing the rubble on Armenia Street, Beirut, 2020.

Protesters near the Grand Theater, Downtown Beirut, 2019.

MARISA MOREIRA SALLES

THE ILLUSION
OF SOCIAL
PARTICIPATION

These are strident times. Differences in perspectives and world-views easily slip into battles—verbal ones, in the best-case scenario. Divergence has given way to hatred; debate, to name-calling. With this state of affairs, it's only to be expected that each societal sect should defend its own causes. The problem is that those causes, however just and urgent, are countless and clashing; one has to shout in order to be heard, and few rallying cries are able to emerge from the din.

The question is, then: how to make a whole out of these many fragments? Tension and anguish are in the air. This fragmented, quasi-tribal scenario has become fertile ground for politicians who feed on aggression, hatred, and confrontation. The twentieth century saw a long string of struggles against multiple strains of authoritarianism. Now, however, the seeds of rupture and backsliding lie in our daily lives—even within those who support the "right" causes and believe that their pain, their struggle, and their truth are more relevant than others'.

We must find it in ourselves to look to our mistakes and learn with them. We must cultivate memory, even—and perhaps especially—of missteps, in order to steer around the danger posed by populism and authoritarianism on the left and right. We must understand that we live together, in the same place, and that the fall of the core civilizational values will be a defeat for us all.

We must sever our reliance on indignant denunciations that provide no transformation, only the illusion of social participation. It's time to leave our trenches and put forth a new pact for civil society, to define what we are and what we want to be.

These answers are not given. We will have to work through them together, and that can only happen if we commit to an alliance for education—not only to guarantee access to quality formal education for all, but also so that we can turn that education toward peaceful cohabitation and democratic practices. Professionals of all fields must build a common field for action, looking to reconcile country and city, science and religion, art and technology. Education is the bridge which can connect the farthest-flung stories and socioeconomic conditions. The public sphere is where that encounter can and should take place.

Our value as individuals and as nations is not dictated by our consumption, but by the quality of our investment in education, research, science, culture, and public spaces. We must reject the irrationality and belligerence fueled by populist politicians who, under the guise of representing this or that ideology, are only defending their own interests.

In the thick of these challenging times, we are given the opportunity for a renewal: a new contract, born of a movement forged by people of all origins, creeds, means, and ideological positions. An awareness of the danger we face can awaken us to the need to knock down the walls that separate us. It is our duty to forge a wide-ranging social compact, creating meeting places and spaces for common living so that all may grow with—and learn from—diversity.

Marisa Moreira Salles is an editor and designer, as well as the founder of BEI Editora, a Brazilian publishing house. She is the co-founder of the think tank Arq.Futuro and the digital platform Por Quê?. She also holds board positions in the São Paulo Art Biennale and in the Dean's Advisory Council of the MIT School of Architecture and Planning.

Cristiano Mascaro, *Popular Ball in São Paulo*, 2010.

ARCHITECTURAL
BEHAVIOROLOGY

The development of industries in the twentieth century has been geared toward the pursuit of "convenience" and providing us a "better life." This has kept us away from organizing our own livelihoods with skill sets and knowledge about local resources, as well as from letting us participate in capitalistic production. But now, the limits of this improvement on our lives have been revealed by the effects of climate change, large-scale disasters, social segregations, etc. We are fully dependent on services provided by industries. Various barriers between our everyday life and local resources have been constructed without our noticing it.

Architectural Behaviorology is our design theory and methodology. Its objective is to rediscover the forgotten values of resources through the lens of ethnography. It tries to find barriers and challenge them in order to create better accessibilities to local resources, and to activate the behaviors of actors, both human and resource-based.

Architectural Behaviorology introduces better understanding of architectural form into the relationship between various things such as nature, humans, and buildings, and their behaviors. "Natural behavior" discusses climate and environmental phenomena including heat, water, light, and earthquake, typhoons, as well as plants and animals. "Human behavior" discusses habitus within different rhythms, daily, weekly, seasonal and annual. "Building behavior" discusses the repetition of building elements in certain areas, typologies, and their genealogy. Behaviolorogy seeks a delightful synthesis of those behaviors within the architectural entity, with sustainable networks of resources as its background.

Actor-Network Drawing (AND) is then produced in order to share these research observations and bridge them to design practice. AND is inspired by Bruno Latour's Actor-Network Theory (ANT), which made us imagine how architectural design can mean opening the black box and making exchange and interconnection happen within society.[1] We often draw AND by hand.

In the last ten years we have developed a practice of "public drawing." It started by illustrating the recovery project for a fishermen's village affected by the Tsunami of the Great East Japan Earthquake in 2011. Architecture students of the Tsukamoto Lab at the Tokyo Institute of Technology, led by Yoshiharu Tsukamoto, had initially been confronted with the inability to

234

produce meaningful projects in the face of the immense emergency in Tokyo. They started by drawing a large format pencil drawing to imagine the reconstruction of the fishermen's village using, as a reference, thousand-year-old buildings around the world, such as the Ponte Vecchio, sites in Dubrovnik, and the Himeji Castle, among others. This drawing was entitled "learning from 1,000 years," since the Tsunami that swallowed the area was referred to as a "once in a thousand years" event. This drawing on an A0 sheet of paper took four students two weeks to produce.

This drawing process allowed us to both dialogue with history and engage in discussion amongst ourselves. We extended this method to illustrate various public spaces designed by Atelier Bow-Wow. The BMW Guggenheim Lab (NY, USA), Kitamoto Station Square (Kitamoto, Japan), and Miyashita Park (Shibuya, Japan) were drawn in the same manner using the concept of "public drawing." The name of this method refers, on the one hand, to the viewer observing public space and on the other, to the act of mimicking negotiations between different actors in public space by different drawers. This method has become more ethnographic as it has been applied to illustrating various public spaces around the world, such as the Hiroshima Peace Memorial Park and the Galata Bridge in Istanbul. It has also been applied to historical cities to draw from the present situation while referencing the history of the place, as in Venice's "Veduta," Rome, and Zurich.

We learned from the "public drawing" experiments that hand drawings make our bodies and emotions interact with what we observe and understand, and encourage us to live together better in the world.

Atelier Bow-Wow is a Tokyo-based firm founded by Yoshiharu Tsukamoto and Momoyo Kaijima in 1992. Yoichi Tamai joined as partner in 2015. Their interest lies in diverse fields ranging from architectural design to urban research and the reconstruction of commons, which are produced, based on the theory called "Architectural Behaviorology." The practice has designed and built houses, public spaces, facilities, commercial buildings across the world.

1   Bruno Latour, *Science in Action: How to Follow Scientists and Engineers Through Society* (Cambridge, MA: Harvard University Press, 1988).

Venice Summer School, "Architectural Ethnography," Public Drawing learning from *Vedute*, Japan Pavilion, 2018.

SIGHTS OF CAPTURE (A DECOLONIAL RECKONING)

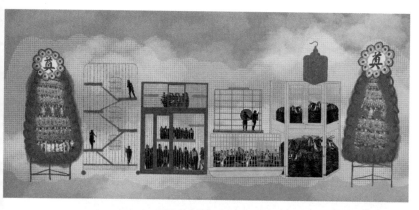

For Hong Kong, any negotiation for a new spatial contract in an age of rapidly intensifying divide must first contend with the architecture of incarceration.

In the film *Prison Architect* (2018) by Cao Fei, a female architect is tasked to transform a museum into a prison. And not just any regular prison. The city's first and most long-lived prison complex under British colonial rule was restored as Tai Kwun in 2018, a major center for art and culture whose mammoth space at the heart of Hong Kong's financial district inaugurated into its renewed grandeur three monuments of the colonial carceral state: the Central Police Station, the Former Central Magistracy, and the Victoria Prison. Commissioned by Tai Kwun itself, *Prison Architect* interpolates two narratives: a female architect ruminates over the ethics of turning the museum into a prison; and a male poet, jailed for penning treasonous verses in the 1967 anticolonial riots, is brutalized by guards. The explicit interrogation of a space of violence brushes up uncomfortably against tantalizing noir shots of the characters amidst the pristine $500 million Herzog & de Meuron re-fabbed vestibules. Reminiscent of Tai Kwun's erstwhile raison d'être as a place of punitive discipline, these glossy interiors would not be entirely inappropriate in a real estate advertisement either.

For the architect and the poet, galleries and prisons both become environments of enclosure, whose long records of punishment and exploitation are as jealously guarded as their attendant experience as sites of cultural production. In one scene, the poet is led to observe an exhibition––the very show the film was commissioned for––and weeps. The architect asks, "So, what kind of prison do you want to live in?" The "humanized" architectural language of the museum papers over the repressive structures of its former selves, but this concealment only begs the question: How do we live with the reality and aftermath of the imprisonment of fellow human beings? If, as Hito Steyerl has already shown, the museum is a battlefield in the wider field of the military-cultural complex, it has perhaps also always been a prison.[1]

The 2019 anti-establishment struggle in Hong Kong has pushed this problem to the forefront of daily life. More than seven thousand protesters have been arrested, of which over a thousand have been charged and 40% are secondary school and university students. Countless people have now endured extraordinary shows of force by riot police, their flesh bearing the aftermath of "less-lethal" weapons deployed with impunity. The unjust deportation of migrants and foreign journalists has directed the public gaze toward the unconscionable conditions of immigrant detention centers and border policing. In a city that already holds the highest number of incarcerated women in the world, the COVID-19 crisis has relied on incarcerated women's labor in producing surgical masks under coercive structures of wage work that long predates the public health crisis.

What this all means is that an entire generation will have been decisively shaped by mass subjection to the carceral architectures of an unaccountable state. As an emerging class of "resistants" pass through these spaces of engulfment, what will new ways to coexist entail in an abolitionist bid to remake the world?

Lausan Collective is a group of writers, translators, and organizers who seek to build transnational left solidarity beyond the dictates of capitalism and the state by holding multiple imperialisms to account. Emerging from the 2019 Hong Kong protests, Lausan believes a radical imagination of Hong Kong's future must center cross-border solidarity based on class struggle, migrant justice, anti-racism, and feminism.

Infinitely scalable, the cage has long been a practical architectural baseline of living and coexisting in Hong Kong.

Carceral labor in the wake of uprising and pandemic falls disproportionately on women in a fractured present overwhelmingly mediated by the screen.

1   Hito Steyerl, *Is the Museum a Battlefield?*, (2013). Lecture and HD video.

THE BLACK
NEW DEAL

It was not until I moved to New Jersey and started working for an institution here that is older than the US government that I understood the meaning of the term "garden" in Garden State. The state motto has been printed on license plates since the 1950s, but even the state's own website refers to the moniker as having a conflicted and vague history. This is because *the garden is the plantation*. New Jersey was the last of the Northern states to abolish slavery completely, phasing out this system of legalized sex trafficking, of extraction of unpaid work under threat of death, only with the end of the Civil War in 1865.

What does this matter for us—for how we will live together this century? This week?

Speculation can operate in different temporal trajectories.

Firstly, what would architectural production look like if architects in the eighteenth and nineteenth centuries had aligned themselves with the abolitionist cause? This would have meant architecture opening a porous relationship between the systematically terrorized craftspeople who built significant buildings in the Americas. It would also have meant architectural techniques— such as graphic scale, section, and line type—colluding with the complex plans of Nat Turner, Harriet Tubman, John Brown and other revolt leaders. Given that the Architectural Institute of America was founded at the precise moment of Reconstruction, when skilled Black laborers might have finally entered the field of architecture...considering this alone constitutes a kind of historical alternative that changes the imagination of the discipline. One thinks of Black intellectual life migrating from the invisible labor implied in the drawing set to the position of author. What skills and techniques might we have, what partnerships and conventions, had the discipline positioned itself differently?

Looking forward from there...

How do we emancipate ourselves—no, revolt ourselves— out of that garden? How do we liberate our spatial imaginaries from that motherfucking plantation, that green cover up, that placid landscape that was never placid, but only ever a place to organize for or against some kind of death threat?

White supremacy and racism continue to be a public health threat in America. As architects and urban designers, let us take this public health threat as seriously as we took the call to "light and air" at the beginning of the last century. Without a century of work defined by that great migration of Black intellectual life from laborer to architect, we face this century and its questions of how to live. How to live in the midst of ecological crisis, the rise of authoritarian governance, and global consolidation of wealth.

Representing, yet again—the injustice we know to be the case—is not enough. We cannot defer the will to act to others. I posit, rather, that architecture can participate in the confronting and even dismantling of an outmoded anti-democratic reality. We must also challenge the violence implied in our discipline's formalization project and understand this in relation to other problems of representation. Let us commit to an architecture of reparations, for the Black diaspora and all the anti-extractive anti-genocidal cosmopolitics of Black emancipation. This is an architecture that participates in the abolition of Whiteness, that continues Henri Lefebvre's call *Toward an Architecture of Enjoyment*. This is a Black New Deal.

V. Mitch McEwen is an architectural designer, urban designer, and founding principal of Atelier Office. Prior to founding Atelier Office, McEwen was an urban designer for Bernard Tschumi Architects and the Department of City Planning in New York City. She is an Assistant Professor at Princeton University School of Architecture. She has been awarded grants from the Graham Foundation, Knight Foundation, and New York State Council on the Arts.

Princeton University Black Box Research Group, *Hot Grandma Chair*, 2018.

M BELÉN SÁEZ DE IBARRA

LIVE
TOGETHER

Through the figure of the shipwrecked refugee or the unwanted migrant, we are overcoming the idea of "the citizen of the world" and revealing that world to be a spoiled utopia, sick with the inhuman idea of sovereignty within which only a few enjoy the promise of being citizens and subjects of rights.

Today, those refugees and migrants are the languid shadow that corporate imperialism casts on the globe. The large-scale biotic extraction of wealth for the few produces and accumulates by way of dispossession, and condemns us to enormous inequality as the essence of what we have naturalized in our social habitat as a model: development, growth, finance.

When climate breaks into our history, we must think about new content for the meaning of living together. We must remember that colonialism is an incessant battle against life, weather, land, and water.

As philosopher Michel Serres proposes, we need a peace treaty with life that permits a deep shift in our consciousness and enables a metamorphosis in which humanity mirrors the sacred.

The pollution and violence that coloniality has produced over life is also a cultural disease, and treating it as such is the first step in laying the foundations for a new biopolitical struggle. The recognition of other ways of knowing allows us to come into contact with the semiotic wisdom of life itself as thinkers of the long-term, where earth, climate, water, plants, animals, and stars all have voices, thoughts, and knowledge. This contact with a deeper time and multitude of ways of knowing allows us to appreciate the notion of life in transit, restlessly transforming and mutating itself. This continuum of other intelligences is an agent that modifies and intervenes in our existing materiality, as well as in the unshaped essence of life.

But we are and have been humans of the short-term and of highly focused specialization. This makes us partly responsible for the global change in the weather, because we invented or distributed the means and the tools of powerful, effective, beneficent, and harmful intervention. We are inept at finding reasonable solutions because we are immersed in the brief time of our powers and imprisoned in our narrow domains.

To face what German sociologist Ulrich Beck has called the "metamorphosis of the world," an enormous exercise of imagination is required. Beck famously coined the term "risk society," and what we must attend to now is precisely risk assessment and control, banning the exploitation of various natural resources, and unwinding of harmful mechanisms, while addressing the issues of common waters, common air, and common lands. The goal is nothing less than the guarantee of equilibrium and compensation for damages suffered at the hands of global capitalist adventurism.

The idea of architecture and urbanism will also suffer this metamorphosis like other disciplinary ideas focused on the anthroposophical. The sociology of living together will finally force us to reinvent the crossings of sciences, biotic notions, and ongoing interactions between other intelligences.

In charge of the Cultural Heritage Direction at the *Universidad Nacional de Colombia,* M. Belén Sáez de Ibarra, directs the Art Museum. Her programs involve collaborative teams in long-term research, such as *Selva Cosmopolítica* (Cosmopolitical Forest), which brings together the arts, heritage, and work with communities in their territories. She is currently working on *Devenir universidad* (Becoming University) lead by Ursula Biemann in the Colombian Amazonia.

M. BELÉN SÁEZ DE IBARRA

Ursula Biemann, *Devenir Universidad,* 2021.

NOAH'S
RETURN

KARIM BASBOUS

The Anthropocene is living its last days, and our civilization is, for the first time, confronting material limitations. It is fitting therefore to question what we now mean by both "living" and "together" as our habitat itself is threatened. How can we contemplate life when everything compels us to organize survival? What is human life without the company of bees and the many other insects and plants that are essential to sustaining our environment? Conceiving the city as a locus of social and urbanistic order isn't enough anymore: "together" must now include the animal and vegetal community without which human life finds itself considerably weakened.

For several decades, our production system has exhibited signs of increasingly frenetic fever—omens of a voraciousness that will leave no parcel of resource unexploited. Its power is draining the very foundations of the city: the pillage of resources appears unstoppable; the privatization of nature by a handful of industrialists has devitalized our vegetables and allowed monopolies to gain control of our seeds; public space is surreptitiously privatized under cover of developing a "smart city" whose sensors will become the best intelligence agents; jobs are disappearing as artificial intelligence develops, while elected officials, at a loss for a solution, hide their powerlessness in a fog of communicational ingenuity; social media rants have replaced ordered civil debate; globalization has perversely exacerbated nationalism; gratuitous violence is multiplying throughout the social body; and a mounting obscurantism is fanning the flames of extremisms of all sorts.

We realize that the gods were merely passing by. As they withdraw, they leave us alone with the Earth. It is now Earth's turn to mete out its retribution. We must ready ourselves for it and envision the foretold Flood as a great bath, one that will cleanse and wash away all that will eventually be called the Old World. We have no choice but to build the Ark, in preparation for a new alliance between Man and Earth, an alliance through which architecture—nowadays too often reduced to surface

Karim Basbous is an architect. He is tenured at the École Nationale Supérieure d'Architecture de Paris-Val de Seine and teaches at the École Polytechnique. His works include *Avant l'oeuvre, essai sur l'invention architecturale*, (Les Éditions de l'imprimeur, 2005), articles in *Le Visiteur*, as well as in journals including *Faces, D'A, Les Cahiers de l'École de Blois, New Geographies* (Harvard), *Albertiana, Le Monde Diplomatique*, and Libération.

vanities and subject to the whims of fashion—will have the opportunity to recover the prestige of a major art, capable of proposing a sustainably inhabitable environment. Our technophile enthusiasms do not exempt us from lending an ear to myths, these very ancient accounts of "fake news," which patiently deliver a salutary truth which no current discourse can ever entirely dismiss.

Translated from French by Joumane Chahine

Bêka & Lemoine, *Acqua Alta a Venezia* (High Tide in Venice), *Homo Urbanus Venetianus*, 2019.

SPOILER ALERT: *YEARS AND YEARS* AND THE PROMISE OF INTERFACE DESIGN

For those who live in cities, togetherness is inescapable. Compressed in small spaces, citizens have found a way to cope with it, and even find pretexts to be proud of the shared hardship. Yet, the continuous friction builds up static electricity and fires sometimes erupt violently, fueled by deep-seated antagonism between established factions living side by side in precarious proximity. Despite all the lore, that togetherness may be hardly tolerated, after all. Designers at all scales—from urban planners and infrastructure engineers to product, communication, and interface designers—can deploy the ammunition in their arsenal to help manage it, while protecting the "significant otherness" (a term coined by Donna Haraway in her 2003 book *The Companion Species Manifesto*) that is at the basis of contemporary culture. Indeed, cultural diversity is as essential to survival (not only of our species but of the whole planet) as biodiversity.

What is the nature of otherness? Is it akin to antimatter, lethal but necessary, trembling on the verge of total annihilation? If conflict is unavoidable, a communicative interface can sometimes help, as evidenced in a 2019 British drama series by Russell T. Davies titled *Years and Years* (a coproduction of BBC and HBO.) The six episodes give a glimpse of the next fifteen years by following the members of the Manchester-based, kaleidoscopically diverse Lyons family as they cope with plausible global events including a Chinese military base on an artificial island in disputed waters; the explosion of a nuclear bomb; and the ascent of a ruthless entrepreneur turned politician (Viv Rook, played by Emma Thompson), her ultra-populism brought to its fateful and tragic apotheosis.

The characters are all extraordinarily compelling—to every viewer their own. Mine is Bethany. Played by Lydia West, Bethany Bisme-Lyons starts out as an awkward and introvert tween and ends up as a glorious and luminous cyborg hero. She can follow her natural evolution thanks to interface design, I reckon, wearing a Snapchat-like "Filter" at first, and then slowly augmenting herself to channel pure data, growing comfortable in her tech-empowered nature. Filter, the screenplay explains, is "a flat panel of graphene IN FRONT OF HER FACE [...] so thin, it's only visible when light catches it at certain angles [...] She's got the setting on DOG, dog ears, nose, a lolling tongue [...] The superimposed elements move with her face. A microphone within the mask makes her voice high and funny." She is still hiding.

By episode five, Bethany has gotten a state-of-the-art software and hardware upgrade. She is not an AI—she still has her body and her beautiful humanity. She explains to her baffled parents "…I keyed into satellites, just thirty seconds ago, so I can see the course of El Niño. And I can tap into pressure sensors along the Atlantic coast. And barometric readings from ships at sea. If I put all that together…I am there. I'm inside it. The tide. The depth of the sea. And the curl of the waves. Within me. And right now, in Charles Street, Pasadena, a 15-year-old girl called Ephanie Cross has written her first song and put it online and she's got the sweetest voice, so when I combine all of that…. It's joy. In my head. It is absolute joy."

If empathy, the ability to *understand and feel* across cultures, genders, races, molecular structures, and beliefs, is the way forward to live together, with other beings and other species, then design and technology can help by providing us with interfaces, both functional and metaphorical. Bethany, transhuman, becomes an angel, able to be one with mountains, buildings, and stars. She saves the day, the country, and possibly the planet.

Paola Antonelli is Senior Curator at The Museum of Modern Art in the Department of Architecture & Design, as well as MoMA's founding Director of Research & Development. Her work investigates design in all its forms, from architecture to video games, often expanding its reach to include overlooked objects and practices. Her goal is to promote design's understanding, until its positive influence on the world is universally acknowledged.

Sahar Khraibani, Reproduction of stills from *Years and Years* showing Bethany's gradual transformation into a cyborg, 2021.

BLOWING
BUBBLES

That we shall live together is certain; *how* is the question. We are already struggling with a world that is made of many different spheres, most of them still permeable, at least to some degree, others resembling bubbles of a rather intangible kind. Many recall those that were on Anton Francesco Doni's mind in the mid-sixteenth century, when it had become difficult to overlook that there was a plurality of worlds, each of these *mondi* different from the others; some "dark," many subject to distant empires, and others so remote they were yet unknown.

That a bubble, like the one we grew in before being born into the open, should remain with us as a nest to which we might return in sickness, in outer space, and finally in death, only adds to the notion of our dependency. Many things are bagged, and some assume the shape of large bubbles. Anish Kapoor's *Cloud Gate* in Chicago takes in everything and gives it back either diminished or inflated; it is perhaps one of those distortion mirrors we need in order to see what keeps escaping us, to gather what wouldn't draw near. An endless sphere, it reaffirms that we are "exposed" in the world and forever in need of a shell, even if it's only a mirage.

The idea of a pod, a return to a flexible bubble haunted Frederick Kiesler, Buckminster Fuller, Mario Merz, Archigram, and many a space freak. Today we must dispense with the ubiquitous plastic bag, preferably translucent, because it litters the land and the oceans. A warning of suffocation was always printed on them. Tomorrow we shall have disposable ones, permeable ones made from potato starch that will disappear as fast as they are produced, but not before uncounted plastic bags of sometimes majestic size hold all the recyclable containers and carry them to their unknown grave. And a grave it must be, for landfills are not like prehistoric mounds of oyster shells and other dormant shapes in the landscape.

Plastic bags stuffed with discarded containers, light in weight and bulky in size, can be carried on one person's shoulders or tethered to a cart. They remind us of a paradoxical experience: what is full leaves only a hollow, embarrassing shell of nothingness that threatens to encrust the world with its superfluity. Reduced to itself and without its contents, containers need to be contained somewhere, not left where they are.

The world bubbles up and we remember that once we were nothing. Now we are learning to live as if we were still in a bubble,

Kurt W. Forster has taught at Stanford, MIT, ETH, The Bauhaus-Universität Weimar, and is a visiting professor at Princeton University. He was director of the Canadian Centre for Architecture, the 9th Venice Architecture Biennale in 2004, and founding director of the Getty Research Institute. He has published books on Pontormo, Schinkel, Warburg, Mateo, Gehry, and is now working on a text with Peter Eisenman.

enclosed in a gossamer film of connections, of viscous and invisible microwaves and distant links to an infinity of others just like us. Doni's *mondi* have infinitesimally multiplied and still we remain just one within them. An accident?

Anish Kapoor, *Cloud Gate*, Millenium Park, Chicago, 2004–2006.

Plastic bags for a gatherer of cans and bottles, New York City, 2018.

Antonio Francesco Doni, Title page of *I Mondi*. Venice: Francesco Marcolini, 1552.

EXPANDED CITIES FOR AN ECOLOGICAL AGE

Since the United Nation's paradigmatic announcement in 2007, we've gotten a little too used to the claim: "75% of the world population will be living in cities by 2050." Many quoted this, almost as a prayer, in every urbanism-related lecture. But while the larger flows of migration still follow that direction, there are also growing signs of the reverse phenomenon.

For some time already, several experiments have been looking towards original ways of understanding territorial expansion and challenging rigid definitions of what is urban or what is rural. The pandemic has catapulted the urge to produce original models that must not only be aware of our relationship to the planet and its consequences, but also provide solutions to essential needs often based in less conventional attitudes.

It is curious that an exhibition such as *Countryside: The Future* was opening at the Guggenheim in New York as COVID-19 hit the world with such force as to make sheltering-in-place a widespread condition. The experience of urban life was annulled, forcing the majority of us to find new habits of production and consumption. Rem Koolhaas's thesis criticizes the global fixation with "Total Urbanization" as a consequence of a capital-oriented society, claiming the need to question it by rediscovering the countryside.[1] But instead, in the blink of an eye, our domestic interiors and screens replaced the streets, offices, schools, and theaters, as well as all other metropolitan representations.

As a consequence, many people are opting to move outside the formal city limits. During the last year, we have relearned that place doesn't necessarily condition all economic relations and the production of a certain goods. We are together reaffirming something that was already there: technology has long ago inaugurated an era of potential decentralization of flows of capital and labor.

But an expanded city model shouldn't be confused with urban sprawl 2.0, or other similar ideals. We cannot leave behind the sustainable aspects of urban density in terms of efficiency, nor can we ignore that cultural diversity is essential for radical transformation. On the contrary, to live together in an expanded city, we must inquire about the validity of the "specific metabolic relation between the cities and their productive hinterlands," as David Harvey put it, and be aware of the complex ecosystems we are forming by exploring the relationships between work, leisure, technology, land resources, and a renewed democratic form of sharing economies.[2] Without intending to, many of us have lately experimented with many of these.

In developing countries, other intricate layers are added. For instance, in Argentina, some politicians are calling for a so-called "return" to rural romanticizing about the idea of a poorer and more just society to face the huge economic emergency that the lockdowns have enhanced. A crucial fact is that most rural contexts in the Global South are defined by their disconnection, lacking access to health, education, and work opportunities. That, together with the outgrowth of poverty and informal settlements that overpopulated cities generate and aren't capable of resolving, shouldn't allow us to be naive.

The idea of "Expanded Cities for an Ecological Age" is not based on any predefined aesthetics. It understands design as a tool capable of intermingling different strata to live together. By "Ecological Age," we are not only incorporating global warming as a primary concern that is fundamental to the great acceleration that extreme modernization derived from, but also calling for an essential transformation in our symbiotic and philosophical relation to the planet.

Florencia Rodriguez is an Argentinean architect, editor and critic. She is the co-founder and Editorial Director of –NESS and Lots of Architecture –publishers.

1   Rem Koolhaas, "Ignored Realm," in *Countryside, A Report*, ed. AMO/Rem Koolhaas (Cologne: Taschen, 2020), 2–3.

2   "Up until the sixteenth or seventeenth centuries, urbanization was limited by a very specific metabolic relation between cities and their productive hinterlands coupled with the surplus extraction possibilities (grounded in specific class relations) that sustained them.... Cities were forced to be 'sustainable', to use a currently much-favored word, because they had to be." David Harvey, "Cities or Urbanization?" in *Implosions/Explosions: Towards a Study of Planetary Urbanization*, ed. Neil Brenner (Berlin: Jovis, 2014), 55.

Pablo Gerson, *Aerial Series*, 2019.

FLORENCIA RODRIGUEZ

AROUND A
BUFFER ZONE
POOL:
"WE" SOLDIERS,
CHILDREN,
PALM TREES,
AND BEETLES

This photo of the 1949 Ledra Palace Hotel and pool on the island of Cyprus tells a fascinating story about the intersection of tourism, politics, and pests: These are all forces coexisting on the physical landscape and shedding light on *who* is "we" in the question "how will we live together?"

One story told by this image is that of a once glamorous hotel built during the twilight of British colonialism. After the island became independent, the Ledra Palace Hotel and its aesthetics of leisure and luxury set the standards for vigorous national plans to forcefully insert Cyprus on the map of Mediterranean tourism hubs during the 1960s.[1]

This photo also tells a story about the current afterlife of the building as the headquarters of the United Nations peacekeeping mission in Cyprus. Located within the "buffer zone" that divides the island, the otherwise abandoned Ledra Palace is a venue for international diplomacy and for Greek and Turkish Cypriot peace negotiations. This decaying building is also home to UN soldiers and their families, and the remnants of children's birthday parties by the pool (red balloons on the right) nearby uniformed soldiers (center) and deserted buildings in the buffer zone right behind (back left in the photo) show the overlaps of everyday social practices with militaristic realities.

There is a third story told by the beheaded palm trees: a story about a tiny, rapidly multiplying, and incredibly resistant beetle called the "red palm weevil," whose arrival in Cyprus less than a decade ago was underestimated by authorities until it infected most of the island's palm trees—a quintessential emblem of beachfronts and other landscapes of leisure around Cyprus, which are now threatened with extinction.

The dying palm trees and uncontrollable pests may appear to create a new material aesthetics between architecture and nature, but they also demonstrate how ecological accidents unexpectedly intersect with diligent socioeconomic planning. Meanwhile, the rather unnatural prospect of a complete elimination of a tree species by the beetle challenges the divisions of the natural and unnatural, the human and non-human, to ultimately shed light on new forms of subjectivity. The beetles, as an aspect of denigrated "nature," or a form of "subnature," give us clues of how we can rethink who "we" are.[2]

If the Ledra Palace once encapsulated development dreams and modern glamour, it is now a locus of geopolitical managerialism and the physical hub of UN's insistent efforts to manage "better futures." The fact that the beetles and palms are creating a very different landscape within the quasi-desolate hotel is not merely ironic; it underlines how any new attempt to imagine "how we can live together" must come to terms with the conditions we (as well as *others* whom we have neglected) have created so far.

Panayiota Pyla is an architectural historian and theorist, with a PhD from the Massachusetts Institute of Technology. She is currently teaching at the University of Cyprus, having previously served on the faculty of the University of Illinois at Urbana-Champaign. Her research and writings focus on the history and politics of development, environment, and modernism.

1 Panayiota Pyla and Petros Phokaides, "'Dark and Dirty' Histories of Leisure and Architecture: Varosha's Past and Future," *Architectural Theory Review* 24, no. 1, (2020): 27–45. https://doi.org/10.1080/13264826.2020.1753282

2 David Gissen, *Subnature: Architecture's Other Environments* (New York: Princeton Architectural Press, 2016).

Ledra Palace Hotel, Cyprus. The pool area surrounded by infested palm trees; a current user (UN soldier) appears in the center back.

HOW CAN
LIFE SURVIVE
DESIGN?

In 1932, Richard Neutra *planted* the 2,000 square foot VDL House in Los Angeles, using interlocking volumes, mirrors, glass walls, patio gardens, and roof terraces filled with sky-reflecting pools of water to demonstrate that a family could live "'humanely" in a small space with expansive views of nature.[1] He sited the house at the edge of the lot to encourage it to *grow* into more houses and subdivided his land into three parcels to facilitate this architectural propagation.[2] Neutra's well-known efforts to make architecture accord with organic life neglected one of its most salient characteristics: that life is subject to limitation, finitude, and death. His understanding of architecture transformed industrialized mechanization and its logic of infinite repeatability into a theory of life without end. Even in 1954, when Neutra published *Survival Through Design* because he had become afraid that the environment was developing "an ominous tendency to slip more and more out of control," he still imagined that architects could "prevent the destruction of humanity" through the unfettered use of biomechanical forms.[3]

In 1997, Leslie Dick wrote "Nature Near," a short story about a year she spent living in Neutra's Strathmore Apartments.[4] In keeping with his theory of architectural propagation, Neutra had strategically oriented the units to give each view the illusion of maximum expanse. His careful design to help more people to live together humanely included an "ant-proof cooler"—a device to safeguard human food by surrounding it with ant-drowning oil. Although a reluctant transplant to LA, Dick's appreciation for the house grew, but along with it so did a mysterious mark on her buttocks. The infection grew larger and more painful until eventually her flesh began to turn black and die. The necrosis was caused by a venomous spider that had been secretly living with Dick in her Neutra apartment. The black recluse, a California desert native, had survived the "thin veneer of greenery" that architects had spread over the land, and entered the house.[5] For Neutra, "living together" concerned humans only, a category error that turned Dick's buttocks, and her house, into what her doctor called "a battle for life and death."

Today, with Neutra long gone, the VDL House is sustained by its use as a site of cultural production and as such it came to be briefly inhabited by a large tortoise named Cura.[6] For *The Arcadia Center*, an installation exploring environmental empathy, the Ben Thorp Brown filmed Cura as she walked slowly around the VDL House, looked out the picture window and even read *Survival Through Design*.[7] Tortoises are abysmally prehistoric creatures, but being invited to imagine one as the subject of a Neutra house conjures neither the geological history before the human that troubled architects during the nineteenth century, nor the life without end that sustained the biomechanical fantasies of the twentieth century; rather, it evokes an ecological history after the human that now troubles architects of the twenty-first century. The conceptual work that is required today is to ask not only how more of us can live together, but also what kinds of beings can be considered architectural subjects, what limits and expansions of the human are needed, and how we can imagine designing Arcadia with life itself in the balance.

Sylvia Lavin is a critic, curator, historian, and theorist whose work explores the limits of architecture across a wide spectrum of historical periods. Some recent books include *Architecture Itself and Other Postmodernization Effects* (Spector Books, 2018), *Kissing Architecture* (Princeton University Press, 2011), and *Everything Loose Will Land, 1970s Art and Architecture in Los Angeles* (Verlag für moderne Kunst, 2013). She is Professor of Architecture at Princeton University and is currently working on a book about trees.

SYLVIA LAVIN

Ben Thorp Brown, *Cura* (still), 2019. 4K Video, 5.1 sound, 17:34 min. As part of *The Arcadia Center*. Co-produced by the Jeu de Paume, Paris; CAPC musée d'art contemporain, Bordeaux; and Museo Amparo, Puebla, with the support of Creative Capital.

1 The VDL House, Neutra's own house and initially his studio, was named after the Dutch philanthropist Dr. Cees van der Leeuw who provided the architect with the necessary financing. On this house and its place in Neutra's oeuvre, see Thomas S. Hines, *Richard Neutra and the Search for Modern Architecture: A Biography and History* (Oxford, UK: Oxford University Press, 1982).

2 Neutra consistently used words and concepts like "growth," "planting," and "life" when describing not only the VDL House but also his architecture in general.

3 Richard J. Neutra, *Survival Through Design* (New York: Oxford University Press, 1954), 24–25, 382. When Sibyl Moholy-Nagy reviewed Neutra's book, she noted that she found his conflation of organic life and machines problematic: "In order to build the best possible polar bear cage, one has to become tremendously interested in polar bears." Moholy-Nagy, *College Art Journal* 13, no. 4 (Summer 1954): 329–331.

4 All the citations in this paragraph are from Leslie Dick's "Nature Near," which first appeared in *Granta* and has been reprinted several times, including in the architectural journal *ANY* 18 (1997): 18–21, and in Terrell Dixon, *City Wilds: Essays and Stories About Urban Nature* (Athens, GA: University of Georgia Press, 2002), 278–286.

5 Spiders played an enormous role in Neutra's architecture: he wrote at length about the human fear of spiders and, borrowing from the work of famed psychoanalyst Otto Rank, developed what he called the "spider leg," a particular kind of trellis that structured the passage from indoors to outside as a therapy. On this psychoanalytic theory and the history and development of Neutra's architectural spider legs, see my *Form Follows Libido: Architecture and Richard Neutra in a Psychoanalytic Culture* (Cambridge, MA: MIT Press, 2007).

6 The house, which had been expanded in 1939, burned to the ground and was rebuilt by Neutra and his son, Dion, in 1965. The house eventually fell into disrepair until it was entrusted to the College of Environmental Design (ENV) and Department of Architecture (CPP ARC) at Cal Poly Pomona, which initiated its restoration. When Sarah Lorenzen became Director of the Neutra VDL Studio and Residences in 2008, the house became the setting for a robust program of exhibitions. The VDL House was named a National Historical Landmark in 2017.

7 Ben Thorp Brown's *The Arcadia Center* was first installed at the Jeu de Paume, Paris, France, June 18–September 22, 2019, where it was part of *The New Sanctuary*, a program devised by Laura Herman. For more on the video portion entitled *Cura*, see the catalog, *Ben Thorp Brown, The Arcadia Center* (Paris: Jeu de Paume; Bordeaux, France: CAPC-Musée d'art contemporain; Puebla, Mexico: Museo Amparo, 2019), which includes my essay, "Who Survives Design?"

FOREGOING
EMPATHY

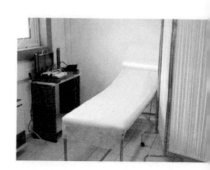

*Living with Other Beings: Foregrounding empathy
and engagement with other beings.*
—Hashim Sarkis[1]

I

On the afternoon of June 10, 2017, Athens Pride—for the
first time in its brief history—occupied Syntagma Square, the city's
central square. Relocating the celebration from its previous
peripheral venues to the country's center of political authority was
itself a forceful claim for visibility and equality; Syntagma Square
stands in front of the former royal palaces of Greece's Bavarian
king, which now house the Greek Parliament. From a little concert
stage overlooking this monumental complex, the Pride organizers,
representatives of LGBT organizations, celebrities, and allies
greeted and cheered the crowd. Nearing the end of the opening
talks, a representative of LGBTQI refugees* took to the stage to
share his own account: he fled persecution back home only to find
himself trapped in homophobic Greece while Europe turned its
back. His observation was resounding, as were our empathetic
sighs, to which he responded: "Save your tears! I don't need them.
What I want is a job and a place to stay."

II

Paul Bloom, a professor of psychology and cognitive science,
explains that empathy is both biased and narrow-minded: people
are prone to feel empathy for those who look like them or share
ethnic and national backgrounds, for example.[2] Moreover,
empathy remains dormant when we encounter statistical data,
large numbers, or climate predictions. It connects us to specific
individuals and nearby events but fails when it comes to the
planetary scale, let alone to atmospheric particles and depleted
aquifers. Nevertheless, there is a persistent and fundamental
assumption that when we do feel the sufferings of others, we are
prompted to relieve it. This alleged drift from empathy to good
deeds has structured Western moral philosophy and politics since
the seventeen hundreds. Rousseau analyzed it under the rubric
of *pitié* (pity) and Adam Smith under that of *sympathy,* but both
positioned it at the center of ethical judgments and actions.[3]
More urgently, empathetic awakening has been the fulcrum of
humanitarian reason: in the humanitarian equation, depictions of
suffering mobilize empathy to solicit donations. These depictions
of the human, to use Michel Agier's term, present life *stripped bare*

in the degradations of suffering, reifying nothing but absolute and essentialized victimhood.[4] Thus, the problem is not what humanitarians call "compassion fatigue"—desensitization due to overexposure to stories and spectacles of suffering—but rather, the acceptance of asymmetry that empathy implies. A world is divided between haves and have nots, benefactors and beneficiaries, where rights, desires, and interests are not enacted and negotiated but donated and bestowed at the beholder's will and benevolence.

III

It is neither a tenable nor a desired pursuit to stop feeling empathy, to stop associating with the agonies and pleasures of *other beings*, to borrow the formulation of the Biennale's curator. Empathy is akin to instinct or reflex, it is what makes art, theater, literature, and cinema work.[5] But empathetic awakening is not the only force that motivates kindness and care. Adrian Piper asked us to break the asymmetry of empathy by sharpening our modal imagination, our capacity "to envision what is possible in addition to what is actual."[6] To be sure, architects have always felt the need to encompass the position of the proverbial users/ inhabitants, real or imagined, of their architecture. This act of architects' empathy is not ethical as such, but instrumental for the sake of architecture's greater professionalization and impartiality. But to make a more responsive, expansive, daring, equitable, and contingent architecture, empathy just can't cut it. Because it is biased, narrow, and asymmetrical, it leads to the design of emergency shelters for "hospitality centers," i.e., prison camps, and eye-catching spectacles for militarized borders to be consumed and celebrated in architectural exhibitions.[7] It transforms protocols of participation, collaboration, and engagement into safeguards for architects' positionality and oft-paternalistic expertise. In Athens, the speaker's utterance was a call for intersectional solidarity that disrupts the asymmetrical modality of empathy. His demand is unequivocal and opens up the possibility for rethinking how seemingly disparate causes—displacement, LGBTQI* rights, and housing affordability—could coalesce into tactics of action and representation. Joining the struggle, without usurping or patronizing it, requires both acknowledging the profession's complicity in systemic injustices as well as decentralizing authority and power, within and without the discipline.

Theodossis Issaias is an architect. Currently, Theodossis is Associate Curator, Heinz Architectural Center, at the Carnegie Museum of Art. Since 2009, he has been practicing as a founding member of Fatura Collaborative, an architecture and research collective. His PhD dissertation, *Architectures of the Humanitarian Front*, (Yale School of Architecture) explores the nexus of humanitarian organizations and architecture and their relation to displacement and conflict during the 1920s and 1930s.

1   Introduction by Hashim Sarkis, Curator of the 17th International Architecture Exhibition, "How Will We Live Together?, *Theme of the Biennale Architettura 2021*," La Biennale di Venezia, 2020, https://www.labiennale.org/en/architecture /2021/introduction-hashim-sarkis.

2   Paul Bloom, *Against Empathy: The Case for Rational Compassion* (New York: Ecco, 2016), 31.

3   Adam Phillips and Barbara Taylor, *On Kindness* (New York: Picador, 2010), 13–45.

4   Michel Agier, "Humanity as an Identity and Its Political Effects (A Note on Camps and Humanitarian Government)," *Humanity: An International Journal of Human Rights, Humanitarianism, and Development* 1, no. 1 (Fall 2010): 30.

5   Namwali Serpell, "The Banality of Empathy," *The New York Review of Books* (blog), March 2, 2019, https://www.nybooks.com/daily/2019 /03/02/the-banality-of-empathy/.

6   Adrian M. S. Piper, "Impartiality, Compassion, and Modal Imagination," *Ethics* 101, no. 4 (July 1991): 726.

7   An indicative example is the installation of pink seesaws between the metal slats of the US-Mexico border wall by the architectural studio Rael San Fratello. The description of the project reads: "[Raphael San Fratello's 2009] Border Wall series approaches the issue with a combination of satire and empathy, reimagining the wall between the two countries as a literal fulcrum on which trade and labor relationships are balanced (Teeter Totter Wall)". See "Rael San Fratello," *The Architect's Newspaper*, April 11, 2014, https://www.archpaper.com/2014/04 /rael-san-fratello/.

Different medical care rooms from eight solidarity clinics across Athens. Fieldwork by Elisavet Hasa, Fatura Collaborative, 2019.

IMAGE CREDITS

page 12
Fondation Le Corbusier, Paris, J 106

page 15
Courtesy A. V. Shchusev State
Museum of Architecture, Moscow

page 21
Photo: Kimberly Dowdell

page 24
Photo: Craig Wilkins
Courtesy Craig Wilkins

page 27
Courtesy Not An Alternative/
The Natural History Museum

page 30
©2019 Marie-Rose Osta

page 33
Photo: Yi Shien Sim

page 36
Photos: Zahira Asmal

page 39
Photo: Ryoji Iwata on Unsplash

page 42
Photo: Susana Hidalgo

page 45
Baihuaeri Waorani Commune,
Pent, Baihua

page 48
(top) The United States Library
of Congress
(bottom) Fernando Santos Granero
et al., eds., *El Ojo Verde:
cosmosvisiones amazónicas*,
2000. Courtesy AIDESEP–
Formabiap, Iquitos, Peru

page 54
The al-Sabah Collection
LNS 298 MS

page 57
Photo 12 / Alamy Stock Photo

page 63
©Instituto Lina Bo e P.M. Bardi

page 66
Print from *Arca Noë* (Amsterdam:
J. Janssonium a Waesberge)

page 69
The Grinnell Collection, Bequest of
William Milne Grinnell, 1920.
Accession Number: 20.120.66

page 72
(top) Kentucky National Guard
Public Affairs Office. CC
(bottom) Courtesy the
photographer

page 76
(top) The Huntington Library,
photCL 396 volume 1 (1). Courtesy
the Huntington Library
(bottom) The Huntington Library,
photCL 396 volume 1 (8). Courtesy
the Huntington Library

page 79
(top) Architekturzentrum Wien,
Collection. Photo: Margherita
Spiluttini
(bottom) Wiener Stadt- und
Landesbibliothek

page 82
*The Roosevelt Island Housing
Competition, New York State
Urban Development Corporation*
(booklet), 1974

page 85
Courtesy NASA Ames
Research Center

page 88
(top) Courtesy the Aga Khan
Trust for Culture and the
CalEarth Institute
(center) Reproduced after the
original by the author
(bottom) Courtesy the Aga Khan
Trust for Culture and the
CalEarth Institute

page 94
©Wikimedia Commons
Author: Andrei Nacu

page 100
Courtesy Arduino Cantafora

page 103
©European Union 2016—
European Parliament. (Attribution-
NonCommercial-NoDerivs
Creative Commons license)

page 106
Photo: Esra Akcan

page 109
Bobulous, CC BY-SA 4.0,
https://creativecommons.org
/licenses/by-sa/4.0, via
Wikimedia Commons

page 112
(bottom) Courtesy The Essex
Institute Historical Collections

page 115
C.V. Starr Virtuai Herbarium,
New York Botanical Garden

page 118
Courtesy the National Museum
of Bahrain

page 121
Photo: M. Christine Boyer

page 124
CCA Commission

page 133
(top) Courtesy Konya
Ethnography Museum
(bottom) Courtesy the General
Directorate for Fine Arts /
Ankara Painting and Sculpture
Museum Collection

page 136
Photo: Hibaa Hutba

page 139
Courtesy the artist,
Galerie Tanit, Beirut, and
Robert Klein Gallery, Boston

page 142
© Eric Staudenmaier

page 145
Courtesy Studio-MLA

page 148
(top) Photo: Daria Scagliola
(bottom) Courtesy
Andrés Jacque/Office for
Political Innovation

page 151
Courtesy the artist

page 157
Photo: Andres Lepik, 2009

page 160
Courtesy of Neeraj Bhatia
©The Open Workshop

page 167
Concept/Design/Curation: Richard
Sommer with Pillow Culture, NYC
(Natalie Fizer & Emily Stevenson)
Photo: Bob Gundu

page 170
(top) Tran Tran
(bottom) Tom Van Eynde

page 173
Courtesy the Aga Khan Museum
of Islamic Art

page 179
(top and center) Photo: Nelson Kon
(bottom) Guilherme Wisnik

page 182
City of Los Angeles, Bureau
of Engineering, Michael
Maltzan Architecture, Inc./
HNTB Corporation

page 188
(top and center) PUB, Singapore's
National Water Agency
(bottom) Ministry of Environment
and Water Resources, Singapore

page 191
(top) Photo: Dinu Lazar on Unsplash
(bottom) Photo: Chromatograph
on Unsplash

page 194
Karl Ludwig Hilberseimer Papers,
Ryerson and Burnham Archives,
The Art Institute of Chicago.
Digital File #070383.
NewRegPattern_p91_ill.140

page 197
top) ©Courtesy of the Humphrey
Spender Archive Collection
(bottom) ©Courtesy of the Mass
Observation Archive, University
of Sussex Special Collections

page 202
Courtesy the author

page 205
Google, ©2021 CNES/Airbus,
Maxar Technologies

page 208
(top and center) Photo: Andy Lord

page 211
IFA Archives

page 217
GOR Ministry of Local Government

page 223
Copyright Saloua Raouda Choucair
Foundation. As seen in Yasmine
Nachabe Taan, *Saloua Raouda
Choucair: Modern Arab Design, An
Exploration of Abstraction Across
Materials and Functions* (Amsterdam:
Khatt Books, 2019), 90–91, fig. 96

page 230
Photo: Cristiano Mascaro

page 233
The Chair of Architectural
Behaviorology, ETHZ

page 236
spf.pdf

page 245
Bêka & Lemoine, *Homo Urbanus
Venetianus*, 2019

page 248
Illustration reproduced after original
image stills by Sahar Khraibani

page 251
Courtesy Kurt Forster

page 254
Photos: Pablo Gerson
Courtesy Pablo Gerson

page 257
Photo: Stelios Stylianou, 2019
©Mesarch Lab

Editors
Hashim Sarkis and Ala Tannir

Authors
Esra Akcan, Noura Al Sayeh-Holtrop,
Mohammad al-Asad, Stan Allen,
Sepake Angiama, Peder Anker, Sarosh
Anklesaria, Paola Antonelli, Zahira
Asmal, Karim Basbous, Merve Bedir,
Aaron Betsky, Eve Blau, Garine
Boghossian, M. Christine Boyer,
Lluís Alexandre Casanovas Blanco,
Pippo Ciorra, Jean-Louis Cohen,
Lizabeth Cohen, Beatriz Colomina
and Mark Wigley, Cynthia Davidson,
Iván de la Nuez, Prajna Desai, Sarah
Deyong, Kimberly Dowdell, Ana
María Durán Calisto, Keller Easterling,
Ross Exo Adams, Mona Fawaz,
Noah Feldman, Kurt W. Forster, Yona
Friedman, Rupali Gupte, Limin Hee,
Samia Henni, Sarah Mineko Ichioka,
Theodossis Issaias, FATURA
Collaborative, Momoyo Kaijima and
Yoshiharu Tsukamoto, Atelier
Bow-Wow, Pamela Karimi, Hamed
Khosravi, Renan Laru-an, Lausan
Collective, Sylvia Lavin, Andres
Lepik, Maria Alejandra Linares Trelles,
Khaled Malas, Didier Maleuvre,
Michael Maltzan, Rania Matar,
V. Mitch McEwen, Rozana Montiel,
Marisa Moreira Salles, Amy Murphy,
Ijlal Muzaffar, Alona Nitzan-Shiftan,
Tosin Oshinowo, Rodrigo Perez
de Arce, Virginie Picon-Lefebvre,
Panayiota Pyla, Nasser Rabbat,
Todd Reisz, Florencia Rodriguez,
Peter G. Rowe, Hussa Sabah al-Salem
al-Sabah, M. Belén Sáez de Ibarra,
Felicity D. Scott, Catherine Seavitt
Nordenson, Richard Sommer, Laurent
Stalder, Hadas A. Steiner, Studio
Folder, Deyan Sudjic, Shirley Surya,
Marrikka Trotter, Alla Vronskaya,
Oliver Wainwright, Delia Duong
Ba Wendel, Sarah M. Whiting,
Craig Wilkins, Folayemi (Fo) Wilson,
Guilherme Wisnik, Gwendolyn
Wright, Ala Younis, Mirko Zardini

Managing Editor
Ala Tannir

Copy Editor
Rachel Valinsky

Editorial Assistance
Kathleen Pongrace

Design
Omnivore, Inc.

La Biennale di Venezia
Editorial Archivities and Web

Head
Flavia Fossa Margutti

Editorial Coordination
Maddalena Pietragnoli

© La Biennale di Venezia 2021

All Rights Reserved under
international copyright conventions.
No part of this book may be reproduced or utilised in any form or by any
means, electronic or mechanical,
including photocopying, recording or
any information storage and retrieval
system, without permission in writing
from the publisher.

Printed on Munken Print White
made out of cellulose from forests
and supply chains run with respect
for the environment, and socially
and economically sustainable

For Italian Distribution
ISBN 9788898727551

For International Distribution
by Silvana Editoriale
ISBN 9788836648610

La Biennale di Venezia
First Edition May 2021

Cover
Michal Rovner, *Current Cross*, 2014.
Video Projection, dimensions
variable. Copyright: Michal Rovner

Printed by
Grafiche Antiga